Dads and Autism

EMERSON DONNELL III

Dads and Autism

HOW TO STAY IN THE GAME

Bond With Your Child,
Develop Affection
And
Keep The Family Intact

AP

Altruist Publishing

Copyright 2008 © Emerson Donnell III
Altruist Publishing LLC
1 Windy Heights Road Suite 102
Califon, N.J. 07830

Orders: www.dadsandautism.com

ISBN: 978-0-578-01901-7

Contents

This book is dedicated to my wife. Through this difficult journey she has proven time and again that she is the stronger gender. Without her, my son and I would have been lost.

I once asked a therapist what is the best thing I can do for my son's condition. "Don't abandon him," I was told, "and the rest will fall in place."

Special Thanks To:

Darlene and Bob Cornell, Paul and Joanne Hurd, Jennifer and Bob Rannells, Uncle Johnny and Aunt Jill, Rich and Sarah Egan, Bruce and Mary Beth Goodman, Dave and Cindy Harper and Susan Morrone. Without your understanding, support and inclusion our journey would be infinitely more difficult. And I'll speak for little Emerson in saying thanks to all his friends, Jonathan, Janelle, Caroline, Kate, Connor and cousin Emily. I know I can't say it, but I love all that we have shared together, from wrestling in the bouncer and riding in the motor cars to swimming in the pool and catching fish. You have helped me understand some of the simple yet most meaningful joys in life.

Also thanks to Rannells Photography, the Studio at Target and Jadwiga Lon.

FOREWORD

Dads And Autism is without a doubt a must-read for any parent, care-giver, teacher and therapist who comes in daily contact with an autistic youngster. This much-needed book is written with a bold and honest disclosure of a first-hand experience and generosity in sharing carefully constructed knowledge of current research and theories on the subject of Autism. The value of the book goes beyond personal testimonial and education, because what is proposed here as a practical training for Dads (and others) is in fact a necessary tool that may have a positive impact on lives of real families. As a professional in the field of Special Education, I would wholeheartedly recommend this great read to any parent or colleague for its usefulness and humanity.

Jadwiga K. Lon,
MA Special Education

Emerson Donnell uses his son as his teacher, about how a father can prevail in the face of autism. Love and dedication inspired this wonderful and helpful book about a father's journey to help his son recover from autism. His book provides a wealth of easy to understand information and helpful hints for other fathers and mothers. It is a must read for parents struggling to break their children through autism's barriers.

Elaine Hardy, MS, RN, APN, C,
Board Certified Family Nurse Practitioner
Holistic Family Healthcare, PC Hackettstown, N.J.

NOTE TO READER

THE ideas, tactics and strategies contained in this book are for educational purposes. It is not intended to replace professional therapies, legal advice or consultations with your physician. All matters regarding your child's wellbeing require medical supervision. The author shall not be held liable for any alleged damages for any information or material provided in this book.

INTRODUCTION

A S with most Dads, I had warm Christmas like visions of my son running to my arms when coming home from a hard day's work. But every night when I came through the door my hands were left empty. My son was deaf, blind and emotionless to my arrival. There was no response whatsoever. His indifference crushed my foundation of fatherhood. After his diagnosis I discovered this was very typical of an autistic child, but it still didn't lessen the pain. Night after night I came home, got into my son's face and vied for his attention. Inside I begged for some response, anything, a quick glimpse back or maybe even a smile, but each night was the same. I couldn't rip him out of his thousand mile stare. I was lost. After another night of irrelevance, I remember tossing my car keys on the counter and cursing under my breath. My evening was ruined again and my behavior was about to set the whole house into another emotional tailspin. Despite my best efforts, I couldn't help but become more detached as hopelessness and depression set in. I had no idea what to do, but I did know if this kept up I would soon be out the door and my family was about to become part of a chilling statistic. Over 80% of marriages that bear an autistic child end in divorce. The reasons are as diverse and complicated as the individual nuances of autism, but like autism there are basic common factors as well. One of the greatest contributing factors to this statistic is a father's inability to develop normal bonds to his child.

So, how can I reach my son who won't acknowledge his name, my face or my touch? Yes, I heard of therapies like ABA and Greenspan, but *how can I get my son to give me a hug when I come home at night? Can't anyone help me with this?* So many other fathers admitted these thoughts to me under their breath. I kept asking therapist after therapist, "how can I get him to acknowledge my presence when I come home from work? How can I get him to give me a hug? How can I get emotion?" Most shook their heads saying this is a hallmark of autism and I would simply have to work through and around it. *How about some specific strategies here?* The closest I got to a 'strategy' was to hold a favorite piece of candy next to my eyes and repeat his name to get his attention, to 'just keep giving him hugs' and he would finally come around. *Was that the best advice they had for me? Get him to look at the candy he wants and hope for a mistaken glimpse in my eyes?*

Though this book can help both parents, the focus is directed toward fathers since we men notoriously have a more difficult time bonding with our afflicted distant eyed offspring. This book gives insight into our frail male psyche, but most importantly it gives dads (and moms) the tools to help bond with their child and develop proper family interaction through a set of discrete affectionate trials or DAT's.

With all that's going on with a newly diagnosed child, the parental need to bond may sound trite or selfish, but the parent/child bond is a cornerstone of whether a family can hold together. Becoming relevant to your child is also the cornerstone for them to develop proper learning ability.

This book is set up as a comprehensive program to first develop yourself as relevant in your child's eyes. From there the exercises provide a foundation to build customary family function. They elicit your child into performing the acts of affection that so naturally come to other children. What begins as meaningless rote drills are designed to blossom back as innate natural displays of family affection. Becoming relevant in your child's eyes is also the very crux of being able to teach other things such as potty training, proper play and language. It also has another great side affect, it helps keep the family together.

Keeping the marriage intact is not only one of the most important things for an autistic child; it's also one of the most difficult things to succeed at under these conditions. My greatest hope is this course of tactics and strategies will work for you and your family. Getting your child to look back with lucid eyes will be the glue that keeps you there working for more. And once you have them here in our world the pathways towards healing will begin.

CHAPTER 1

ALL THE SIGNS WERE THERE AND DADDY'S GROWING DISTANT

FIRST, let me introduce myself. I'm Emerson Donnell. Born and raised in New Jersey, I waited until my 40's to have a child. Little did I know I was a perfect match, a statistical poster child of the typical parent who sires an autistic child, (an older white male living in New Jersey, the state with the highest incidence of autism.) And little did I know after the birth of my son Emerson, "little Em" that my wife Jen and I were being railroaded right into the next statistic. Over 80% of marriages that sire an autistic child end in divorce.

This statistic could be blamed in a myriad of things, but for me and I think for many other dads out there it can be summed up in one word: Frustration. Coming home and not being able to bond with my child in any sense of the word lead to the disintegration of all other aspects of my household. As I educated myself, I read again and again how the odds were stacked against me and my family coming out of this whole. Furthermore I found little out there to help dads in dealing with this crisis in a productive manner.

As a therapeutic exercise I began writing down notes on what worked on helping my son and me to bond. It kept me focused and assisted me in tracking any progression. Soon I began to compile a list of tactics and strategies that were having great positive effects on little Em and our relationship.

The inspiration to make this into a book arrived when a therapist came to our house to observe and assist us in interacting with Emerson. I proudly showed her the nightly greeting ritual I developed in which I elicit little Em to participate. It involves ABA tactics while reinforcing the mantra of Greenspan which is illustrated later in the book. The therapist asked where I learned this strategy. I told her I put it together myself and that it had a profound effect on improving Emerson's behavior when I came home. Not to mention the great effect it had on my overall outlook in being able to handle my son's condition. She asked if she could use the same tactics in training other parents. It was then I realized there really wasn't much out there to specifically address rebuilding the family core and developing affection after diagnosis.

I know I don't have the formal education or training of a professional psychologist or behavioral therapist. But what I do have is the eye to eye empathy and understanding of what you are enduring. I am in your shoes, they just have a few more miles on them. I have had the same angst in my heart, the same pain and the same tears. I am a father of an autistic child, and as a father I have doggedly dug down and found tactics that may help your child start emerging from his or her shell. Most importantly this book is specifically designed to weave the family fabric back together. These aren't tactics to teach your child to match colors, stack blocks or point for food. These are exercises to make you relevant in your child's eyes and to develop and build the affectionate family dynamic as it should be. As a side effect, becoming relevant will later help you teach your child other fundamental necessities.

In this chapter I will spend a short amount of time on my son's background and condition. I will also delve into some of the emotions that go through most men's heads at this stage of discovery. But before doing that I would like to answer the one question that's probably burning through your head that none of the doctors are willing to answer. *Is there hope?* I would like to illustrate that I have seen very disturbing behaviors in children that I originally thought had no hope of living a normal life turn a corner. Head banging, violent temper tantrums, loud repetitive grunting, indifference, even self mutilation are just a few of the more disturbing traits. But with consistent undaunted efforts by parents and therapists I have witnessed dramatic progression.

Please realize one thing about autism. It is a malleable condition, especially if caught and addressed during the early years from ages 2 to 6. In other words with intense therapies many of the terrible behaviors, delays and problematic nuances of autism can be minimized or even reversed. You must approach this as an intervention. Like any other family member who may be lost to addiction or other behavioral problems, the only way stop their fall is to get completely involved and it must be approached with all urgency as this small window of opportunity is omnipotent. If taken advantage of the first couple years of intense therapy can enable the child to have an exponentially greater chance of getting mainstreamed by first or second grade and progress onto a normal lifestyle. However, if ignored, it can mean educational and emotional delays, behavioral problems and social awkwardness for the rest of your child's life. This is why it's so important for fathers to stay the course and plow forward. But the proper tools need to be put into your hands and the techniques taught as soon as possible. Without them, you will flounder and so will your child.

I remember one therapy session I recognized a little boy. Months before, he had no vocabulary, no eye contact and would shriek and flap his arms as the mother constantly struggled to decipher his needs and keep his destructive behavior at bay. When she set him down he would immediately flip chairs, bolt from other children and fight her embrace when she tried to curb him. Last I saw her, she looked as though she hadn't slept in weeks and I could tell her eyes were swollen from crying. I recognized it because I had the same glassy stare and darkened rings when I looked in the mirror. But this time she seemed more relaxed and didn't have the kung-fu grip on her son's forearm I remember from before. The boy turned around, looked at his mother and politely said, "Juice?" I was floored, my mouth was literally agape. I've seen other parents react with quiet envy, but for me, this was a bolt of sunlight cutting through the dark cloud that had formed over me since my son's diagnosis. There, in this little boy's blue eyes was hope staring right back at me. Hope smiled, and then turned away with a bashful grin. *Oh my God, not only was I getting eye contact, but facial communication!*

I couldn't help myself. I touched the mother by the arm. "Excuse me, I remember you from a while back, and I just have to say I can't believe the progress your son has made."

"Oh, thank you."

"What did you do?" I prayed for The Answer, The Silver Bullet. Was she going to tell me it was the gluten free diet, the b-12 shots or Chelation?

"Hard work," she replied. Her eyes set to the glossy stones I remember from the last time I saw her. "Whether it's me, the therapist or my husband, everything we do revolves around getting him to come out of his world and into ours. Also, we got some neighborhood kids and parents involved in helping our son to learn to play correctly. Integration is important for our son. The trick is finding some understanding parents willing to work with you. But don't be surprised if some treat your son like he's a leper." The woman still seemed exhausted, but smiled proudly to my still widened eyes. "He has come a long way," she admitted, "but everything you do with him has to be approached as therapy." She combed her hand through her son's blond hair. "Also, get a good doctor to check out your son's allergies. Lots of these kids have autoimmune and allergy issues that really do affect their behavior. I'm not saying any one thing works, but I bet you'd be surprised about some of your son's chemical imbalances if you ran all the tests."

This was the closest I got to anyone ever showing me light at the end of the tunnel. Any therapist or doctor I asked before never gave us hope. I would constantly ask, "What's the prognosis?" They would turn away, stare in the distance and mumble some indiscernible words. I think the doctor's themselves developed a sudden case of autism. I'm not saying this child was 'cured', but for the first time I saw A to B results of good therapy and parenting. As a Dad and as a human being, that was all I needed to see. For the first time I felt like I could tangle with autism - and win.

Mentally gaining control of my son's condition was an epiphany of sorts. It enabled me to let go of despair and fear and let faith in myself, my wife and my son take hold. Gaining mental control is imperative for any parent to hang in there and keep fighting. Don't get me wrong, your forced endeavor will be an epic battle filled with tiny victories and overwhelming defeats. Know that this ebb and flow of emotion is normal, but the rewards down the road can be priceless.

Stay in there. Autism is bendable.

Recently I have heard Jenny McCarthy declare her son as "cured" and for that she has received a-lot of flack. However, there now is evidence that such a thing is possible in certain instances. Since this condition has taken a front seat, scientists have had the opportunity to view children's progression over the years. Using MRI scans they can compare brain function from an early toddler to teenager. Remarkably, in certain cases they found that the speech and communication centers had rewired themselves to perform as a normally functioning brain! Did this come naturally or was it due to the intense therapy these individuals blossomed from? The common factor I've observed is the parent or parents professed of an intense therapy regimen when their child was first diagnosed. There is scientific evidence that intense therapeutic interventions started at an early age can have profound positive effects. Furthermore, as I will discuss later, there is evidence mounting through the new science of epigenetics as to why this condition is so malleable.

Now, I completely understand with all that you are enduring, your time is valuable and your tolerance thin. I will not spend an inordinate amount of time talking about Little Em, but I must use our situation as a reference point to illustrate what many Dad's go through and how the therapies later worked. So, let's start at the beginning. To our surprise my wife Jen had just given birth to a healthy eight pound four ounce boy. During her pregnancy the amniocentesis failed to find a stem on the apple so we assumed we were having a girl. My grandfather bears the same name so when the doctor announced we had a boy in the delivery room, I had to take seat. The nurse thought I was about to pass out. Maybe I was, but I was over whelmed with the notion of carrying on a legacy. Not that I wouldn't love a little girl, but what can I say, I'm a guy's guy. Besides, we could always try for a little girl next, or so I thought. We named him Emerson Bradford Donnell IV, 'Little Em' for short.

I was so naïve, I thought he should be crawling around like a baby in one of those pampers commercials right way. But as the days then the weeks went by, I was immersed in Baby 101 like any other new parent. Much was normal; however, when a friend of ours had a little girl within three weeks of our boy, I immediately noticed a difference.

Now, studies have shown infant boys to be very different from infant girls from the start. Little girls respond to faces and make much better eye contact, where boys tend to be attracted to 'things', especially shinny things. So, when my little guy didn't respond to my face or my voice everyone said it was normal and I patiently waited for him to come around.

This is where things are very different between moms and dads when it comes to connecting with offspring. Ask a man what his first thoughts are when his baby is born in that delivery room and he will inevitably fast forward through the infancy stage right into toddlerhood. They envision throwing a ball with their little guy or how 'daddy's little girl is going to have them wrapped around her pinky finger.' They don't fondly imagine midnight feedings or changing explosive diapers. So, many men unconsciously keep one foot out of the emotional pool as they wait for that time when their baby becomes a little person.

The problem usually begins when day after day, month after month and year after year goes by and the feedback never comes from your child. I'll admit I was counting the days until Little Em would look me in the eyes and say 'Dada.' I couldn't wait for that connection; to say hey, he's mine! I'm his Dada! And day after day when it never came I knew deep down all the tentacles of bonding were not out and surrounding my son. I needed feedback more than I realized, and as we failed to bond I was feeling guilty that I was viewing this beautiful little boy less and less as mine. Jen wasn't receiving any affection from him either. It was also no help that he was severely colic, crying for hours and hours at a time. We did all we could, changed formulas, coddled and rocked him as much as possible, but if this boy could grow thorns when we touched him – he would. We had no idea why he didn't want to be held, why he was so cranky and unresponsive. Allergies, colic and eczema were little hints of autism tipping its hand.

When he wasn't crying it was still impossible to cuddle and play with him. He wanted nothing to do with us. As a result Jen was becoming more agitated and quiet. We weren't talking so much. We were just sitting, waiting and like our son, cocooning ourselves in our own worlds. Autism is so insidious. It can seep into a household and fray the seams of marriage before you even know it's there.

When my son was first born I remember telling my wife, "He doesn't look me in the eyes. I feel like I can't connect with him." I tried holding him, but it was always all elbows and knees; he was crawling out of his skin trying to get out of my arms. I thought these feelings were of me being an awful dad and I couldn't shake the oil vs. water feel I got every time I held him. I felt terrible, like it was entirely my fault until I held my neighbor's daughter for the first time.

Born within three weeks of Emerson I figured I would get the same distant stare. But she looked me straight in the eyes, reached up and grabbed the tip of my nose. I smiled and she smiled back, something I had yet to experience from my son! My heart pushed tears to my eyes; she was like a babbling brook in my arms, serenity incarnate. I could not believe the wonderful emotion that spilled from the center of my chest when her oversized eyes met mine. This is what I had been waiting for, this is what I had expected parenthood to be, but it was not from my child! I handed her back and immediately picked

Little Emerson back up. The tingling fronds of affection were still there and maybe somehow they would reach out and just maybe Little Em would do the same, look me in the eyes and all would be right in the world.

But when I picked him up he was static electricity of knees and elbows, struggling in my arms like I was handling him with sandpaper gloves. Little did I know at the time, but autistic children typically have an aversion to touch. My arms probably did feel like sandpaper.

Again, I tried to relegate all this to his gender and was reinforced by our parents, the pediatricians and everyone else around us that "he's all boy and there's nothing to worry about." But after experiencing those few moments with that little girl in my arms I was more determined to connect with my son and I was also concerned that something was very wrong.

At 12 months I remember calling his name while he sat in his high chair next to me at the breakfast table. No response. I said it again this time with grit in my throat, but again no response. Again I spoke with more anger, but I did this on purpose. Normal developing children have an innate ability to read anger or frustration, a higher pitch or louder volume as something to stop and pay attention to. But not my son, he didn't flinch. I wasn't just being ignored; it was like I wasn't speaking at all – again another common trait and warning sign of autism.

My wife stopped eating to observe his disregard. By now I was truly frustrated and upset. I coddled his little cheeks in my hand and turned his face to look at me. I drew closer wanting so badly for him to look at me with his beautiful ice blue eyes, but they rolled white into the back of his head. I looked to Jen who saw the same thing I did. *Oh fuck*, I said to myself. I let him go and his eyes came back but turned as far from my direction as possible. I got closer again and his eyes rolled back up. My stomach sank as I returned to my chair and neither of us said a word. Was it denial, fear or heart break? It was all of the above.

We had no idea what we were dealing with but we were seeing all the early signs of autism. Other signs became more apparent as time went on. No response to his name, ignoring a parent walking in a room after not seeing him all day, crying fits, no vocabulary, indifference or aversion to people, however, overly focused on wheels, whether they're on a toy, a vehicle or his stroller.

We questioned our pediatrician as we got medication to treat his ongoing eczema. "No, he's just a boy. They typically develop later than girls." We weren't asked why we were concerned, what was it about our son that made us worry. Nope. In fact, we brought it up to more than one doctor in the pediatric group we worked with. There was nothing more than a once over like kicking the tires of a used car, a reassuring if not patronizing pat on the back and a co-pay on our way out the door. The doctor didn't notice that I was an older father (older parents have higher incident rates of siring autistic children), living in the state of New Jersey, (the state with the highest incidence of autism in the country) that my son being a boy had a 1 in 94 chance of a diagnosis, that he had many allergies and digestive issues, no eye contact and no vocabulary at 18 months. My God, when I think back autism did everything but stand up and kick him in the balls.

Ironically there was a Developmental Milestone sign in the waiting room saying, 'Is your child progressing at the right pace?' It listed the age and the appropriate development level for 12 months, 18 months etc. Neither doctor tried applying this tool.

Unfortunately, my experience with most pediatricians is they are good for runny noses and vaccination schedules. That's about it. Not even ear infections fall in their realm of expertise. I'm sure there are great and vigilant pediatricians out there, we just happened to have this unfortunate experience.

Our son had several ear infections within the first year and half of his life. We were being double whammied and didn't even realize it. Our son's response to sound went from minimal to nonexistent. My wife brought him to the pediatrician twice and we were told there was no infection and his ears were clear. After the second visit my wife insisted on a referral for an E.N.T – an ear nose throat specialist. Her instincts were telling her different and she wasn't going to take the doctor's word.

Turns out both his ears were full of fluid to the point his ear drums were distended. The ENT said it was worse than trying to hear someone talk while under water. At one and a half years old, we thought this explained his speech delay and indifference to our voices. We had our smoking gun! Tubes were put in and we were promised in thirty to sixty days he would be a completely different child.

The operation was in February 28th – at 18 months. Thirty days later there was minimal change. His demeanor was better – obviously he was no longer in constant pain, but his development was still at a standstill. By April we had the therapist from Early Intervention begin testing. At twenty months he was functioning at about the ten month development mark. No one could 'diagnose' autism until two years so it was simply referred to as developmental delays. Without a true diagnosis we were still in the dark and in hopeful denial that he would come around. The 'A' word was something everyone avoided like the plague.

Other parents and friends referred us to Early Intervention. "It's free!" We were told, and the earlier he got help the better. Well, it was free. New Jersey leads the country in a couple of realms. It's the state with the highest property taxes, the highest incidence of autism and it's also one of the few states in the entire country that now charges families for Early Intervention services. New Jersey's Early Intervention Program has a 'Family Share Plan.' Sounds friendly doesn't it? But it's a program that charges families stricken with autism for therapy on a child less than the age of three. Based on the family's income, we now had to open up our tax returns to the State Early Intervention Program. I felt like I was in a proctology exam, except these weren't doctors. Worse yet, the country's financial meltdown had begun and I was in the financial industry. The company I worked at for eleven years shut down in January and I was struggling at a small two man shop. My income dropped by more than eighty percent within six months and Early Intervention now wanted to charge us something in the realm of $800 per month (based on the prior year's earnings) for therapy on a diagnosis of 'developmental delay.'

Though already throttled by the highest property taxes in the country, New Jersey - which also bears the highest rate of autism - effectively dumps the financial burden directly in the laps of parents who are now struggling with the emotional chaos.

Well, after getting that news without anyone hinting at the 'A' word, we opted for a speech therapist and managed to get it covered by our insurance. At the time we didn't think we were selling our son short. We imagined it was just taking longer to recover from his temporary deafness. Early Intervention didn't give any specific diagnosis other than 'he has speech and behavioral delay.' So we hired a speech therapist to work with our son twice a week.

After a month the therapist sat my wife down. "We need to talk," she said. She took my wife's hand. "I am not a doctor, but I am coming to you as a mother and a grandmother. I am coming to you as a friend. Your son has a problem. Again, I'm not a doctor but I think Emerson is in the autistic spectrum."

Jen bawled in her office and admitted later she was angry with the therapist, but knew deep down this woman was onto something. All the barriers of denial and dismissive waves from the pediatrician's and family washed away. "I don't know what to do," she cried.

"I will keep working with him, but you need to set an appointment with a neurologist as soon as possible." We were three months from his second birthday. Neurologists normally won't see a child until twenty four months, however, most are booked three to five months in advance. "The clock is ticking on your son," she said. "You need to set an appointment now. The earlier he gets clearly diagnosed and gets help the more hope he'll have."

Some who read this may say, "shame on the therapist! She's not a doctor and she overstepped her bounds by proposing a diagnosis."

I say thank God for this woman.

No one else put themselves out there. Not the pediatricians, not the Early Intervention evaluators. Looking back it seems everyone was afraid of 'the A word.' It was taboo. Maybe they were afraid after a parent previously lashed out. But as far as I'm concerned this speech therapist handled it perfectly. She was only concerned for our son. Right or wrong in her opinion, her intention and her heart was in the right place. In my opinion the pediatric industry needs to step up as well. A developmental milestone checklist should be made a mandatory part of a semiannual check up. If the milestones are not met within certain parameters, then the child should be automatically referred to a neurologist.

Due to a cancellation, my wife managed to schedule the neurologist for three weeks prior to Little Em's second birthday and we waited. Like most fathers, I didn't want to believe there was anything wrong with him. And each day that I came home to his distant dysfunctional behavior I made the same mistakes and had the same disappointment. I had no idea what I could do to correct his indifference, to make my voice or the sight of my face meaningful in his eyes.

In a way it was like my son never really arrived. There was a child in my wife's arms when I came home every night. He ate at my table, kicked and cried when I tried to pick him up and he kept me up at night. But other than some similarity in appearance, there was less and less for me to connect to. He wasn't growing into knowing his father and I wasn't growing into knowing him. He wasn't coming to me for affection; he was head butting me under the chin when I tried to sit with him in my lap. I was becoming increasingly frustrated, distant and worst of all, I couldn't help myself.

In the meantime my wife and I were growing more distant from each other as she focused more and more on our son. She and I didn't know it, but she was doing what many moms do, becoming the consummate altruist, unconsciously and completely giving up self for her child; what I will affectionately term as a "Mama Bear." Mother bears are well known for their fierce defense in raising their cubs. They will go without eating, let their cubs have first dibs on the kill and fearlessly sacrifice themselves against marauding males.

Many mothers of autistic children instinctively hunker down and become similar fierce single minded defenders of their offspring. All sense of normalcy and self shuts down as the air within the household fills with angst and desperation. Tunnel vision on therapists, theories, diets and schools takes hold as preservation of self and marriage becomes secondary if not meaningless. Like mother bears, they become the single self sufficient parent whose entire being evolves into caring for their cub. They take control of the situation as a man would take control when you get a flat tire on the side of the road. It's a fantastic natural instinct that has helped perpetuate the survival of our species, but it has its consequences.

Dads on the other hand tend to shut down. They get lost and seem unable to absorb all the new terminology and theories thrust upon them when they come home from work. If they are absorbing the situation, they do so in silence. The paradox here is they've become the stereotypic helpless woman on the side of the road while their wives have rolled up their sleeves and dived in. As dad becomes distant, mom starts to feel more alone in this forced venture. She lets go of her husband as if he's simply another object in the way, a distraction that must be put aside just like her own wants and needs. She feels justified in doing so, after all she's not asking her husband to sacrifice any more than she is. This unfortunate yet all too common downward spiral between husband and wife will be addressed later in the book because this typical dynamic can unwind a marriage at frightening speed.

I tried talking to some separated dads, but as one can imagine it's nearly impossible to interview a father whose family has been eviscerated by autism. How can I get a straight answer from someone so ashamed, distraught and confused? On the few occasions I got to talk to such a person they never had any profound answer. The darkness of their thoughts would pull their gaze down towards the ground, their back would give way to the weight of emotion and they would just say, "I couldn't take it anymore" or "my wife just took over, and soon there was resentment and…" An attempt at an explanation would always end in an incomplete sentence and a sigh. That was about as insightful as it got. It was impossible to confront the depth or mechanics of their hopelessness. What I did get out of those fleeting conversations and from my own inner thoughts was they truly wanted to help, they wanted to love their son or daughter and most of all they wanted to be loved back. They just didn't know how to go about it.

The sinister nature of autism is that it not only steals the child from its parent's arms, but it can emotionally devour the entire family. Taking this apart, you can see the common thread as to why estranged fathers leave. They had all lost control and hope in their child, their marriage and in themselves. They tried to swallow autism whole - figure out how to fix it all at once, but unfortunately their will and the marriage broke under insurmountable pressure.

How do we stop this cycle? The answer: Take it in small doses and work on what gives you the greatest reward first. Here's a good analogy of what you're up against. Imagine getting a professional grade jigsaw puzzle dumped in front of you and you're now being asked to simply put it together without any experience or instruction. There are pieces everywhere and you can't imagine where to begin. You pick one piece then another; the odds of finding the mate to that one piece in your hand is a million to one, (Oh and did I mention the room is only lit by one dim 25 watt lamp from across the room?) You soon grow over-whelmed, frustrated and weary - and you walk away. But if someone sat with you, turned up the light and gave you a fundamental process that worked for them, chances are much better that you would be able to sit and begin to make progress.

Autism is The Great Jigsaw Puzzle. Yes, every child's puzzle is different, but to solve them, each puzzle must be approached with similar methodical small exercises and tactics to make progress. You don't attack the puzzle as a whole (looking for a single piece to fit another), instead you divide the tasks to solve autism into small groups. You must separate the edges of the puzzle in one pile, the blue sky in another and flesh tones in another and so on and so on. Start to work on the parts that give you the greatest reward. In my experi-ence, the exercises that prove the greatest reward involve the simple affectionate dynamics of a family. Small successes help keep you in the game, especially ones that further parent child bonding and this is how I've approached the tactics in this book. The pieces of the puzzle you're going to compile and piece together here will be: proper affectionate behavior, proper emotional response and family bonding.

For now, believe through other's example that your child will progress beyond what you can see. As you begin to employ tactics to elicit affection and proper emotion, you and your child will start to naturally develop the bonds you have always hoped for. Furthermore, as will be discussed later, keep your fingers to the pulse of your marriage. It may seem like a selfish exercise or a distraction from your child's needs, but keeping marriage intact has everything to do with helping your child through this.

Synopsis:

Change your mindset from despair and loss of control to belief in your child and your own ability to help him. Understand that with the right guidance, your child will progress in ways you can't imagine right now. Once you begin to exercise systematic strategies to instill affectionate behavior, you will naturally gain control of your situation and start to build the ties that will forever bond you and your child. I know your time is precious and your endurance thin, so to maintain a quick pace of the book I opted to put the charts of developmental milestones as well as red flags for autism in the back for reference. If you bought this book, then you're most likely already familiar with them.

CHAPTER 2

THE DIAGNOSIS

AT the behest of the speech therapist my wife set up the appointment with the neurologist. Emerson was twenty three months old, the earliest any neurologist would schedule an appointment. Their reasoning is a child is not developed enough prior to two years for an accurate assessment. But what most parents don't realize is that most neurologists are booked four to five months in advance. If you suspect anything, book an appointment early. You can always cancel.

The three of us were placed in a cramped room with the neurologist. "Call your sons' name five times." I was eighteen inches away from Little Em's ear as he was immersed in spinning the wheels of a toy train. The neurologist clarified herself further. "Each time you call his name say it louder."

Despite the 'oh f---' moment I had weeks earlier with my son's eyes rolling white in his head, I was still in denial up to this point. My inner voice kept relying on the pediatricians, parents, and friend's reassurances. *"He's a boy, they develop slower. Don't worry, he'll come around."* Sound familiar?

"Emerson, Emerson," no response. "Emerson!" I said louder as my jaw muscles clenched. Little Em kept playing, there was not a wince of auditory discomfort or a glance to even acknowledge my presence. "Emerson!" I blurted, "Emerson!"

Nothing. A chill ran up my back as the neurologist looked down and began writing furiously. To this day I think she did that just so she didn't have to look me in the eyes. It was the turning of the worm for me. The otherworldly feeling pricked my cheeks like they had just been slapped and overwhelming confrontation with the A word sunk into my chest like a knife. Autism's shadow darkened the room like a monster looming between me and the sun.

As we tried to help him with puzzles, keep him from thrashing his arms, the neurologist busily jotted down notes. All the reassurances from friends, family and pediatricians that our son was fine were slashed with every stroke of her pen. And within the confined space of the assessment room my son became increasingly agitated. He began to literarily climb the walls. We didn't understand it then, but he was becoming over stimulated and frustrated.

She added up the scores on her matrix as we tried to reign in our son from destroying the room.

"Well, your son has P.D.D. N.O.S, which is short for Pervasive Developmental Delay, Not otherwise Specified." Then it came. "It's in the autistic spectrum. Your son has mild to moderate autism." The 'A' word took my breath.

"How bad is it? Will he get better? Will he ever be normal?" These were the questions machine gunning from me even though I had yet to fully catch my breath.

The neurologist shook her head aimlessly and shrugged her shoulders. "It's too early to tell." This is where the adrenal glands squeeze. Where's a handbook? How can I fix this? All the fuzzy warm thoughts of father and son fishing, playing ball, going to his peewee games all were shucked from that hopeful place in my mind. "But I will say this," she pointedly said. "Do all you can now. You're ahead of the game for catching this so early and its imperative you immediately get him all possible therapy." She read our gaunt bloodless faces. "Don't think about saving for college."

"Why?" I asked.

"If you don't do anything about this now, he'll never go."

My wife and I were silent in the car. We hadn't said a word since shaking the doctor's hand goodbye.

"Well, you were right," I finally said breaking the ice. "But the doctor said he's in the 'mild to moderate spectrum' so I think he's going to be okay." I was expecting her to melt into tears, but her lips stayed pursed as she focused on the road. "Don't worry, he'll be okay." I said again hoping for some feed back while trying to convince myself at the same time.

Her lack of emotion rattled me. Looking back I can now imagine how a woman must feel when her husband shuts down. The unknown thoughts of what is creeping through your spouse's head can really be unnerving. *Was she going to abandon him, had she checked out? I can't handle this on my own. What am I going to do?*

The fear only lasted a moment, but it's one I don't care to revisit and it's a feeling I never want to convey to her.

Jen dropped me off at my car. We parted without a kiss or a tear from either of us. I began heading back to the office with every intention of going through a normal work day, but on the way I'll admit the first person I called was my mother. I had been brave up until this point, put on the strong face, but when she answered the phone I began blubbering. "Jen was right," I announced as she picked up the phone. "He has autism." It was all I got out before I bawled in the deep grotesque way grown men do only a few times in their lives. I had to hang up the phone and was ashamed for losing my senses. I never made it to the office and cried the rest of the way home.

Jen, however, drove our son back to daycare and went straight to work. To this day I don't know where she found the fortitude. It was one of the many instances to come where she would prove to be the stronger person.

CHAPTER 3

WHY DO DADS LEAVE?

HERE'S a short tongue in cheek letter I once wrote off the top of my head. I tend to apply humor and sarcasm as my tools of coping, but I think much of this has an air of truth to it.

Dear Jen and all the other wives out there coping with autism,

I can't say what I'm feeling so here is a letter of admission. Please understand our male brains have been drenched in testosterone since the day of our inception and as a result they are now irreversibly damaged. We are plagued with delusions of being able to fix anything without directions and truly believed we could control the outcome of any parental circumstance with a stern glare and deep commanding voice. When our precious little gift was born our heads swelled with visions of grandeur. We were going to be the best fathers ever known to mankind. But when we faced the unfixable, the uncontrollable, with the 'A' word - we panicked. The irresistible drive for fight or flight has overwhelmed our being. We've been shaken to our core to imagine our little child may never be 'daddy's little girl' or our 'little buddy.' Worse yet, as we try to cope we are God smacked by the reality of our shallow limits, thin patience and Neanderthal thought process. Finally, we are ashamed as we realize we are blunt instruments

*unable to withstand a fraction of what you can tolerate in raising
a child with special needs.*

Forgive us ladies for we know not what we do.

So why do dads leave? At what point do men give up? Is it when
we get the diagnosis? How long do most guys hang in there? What is it
about our gender that makes us disappear? Are we genetically predis-
posed to flight? Is it the social system in which we live in? Is it the
lack of connection with our offspring at birth compared to the female
gender? Is it a lack of maturity? Is it the amount of testosterone in our
bodies that shortens our patience and allows us to become frustrated
earlier? Is it possible the husband leaves only after being left behind by a
wife who takes control or is it a combination of all these dynamics that
make men take flight?

As autism afflicts each child differently, the reason why one man
leaves differs from one father to the next. But like autism, there are
common threads that tie them together. The biggest common thread,
the inability to connect or bond with his child.

Day in and day out I would come home and announce my arrival
but little Em wouldn't even glance my way. I walked over, called his
name again and couldn't pull him out of his thousand mile stare. Sound
familiar?

"He's busy eating." My wife would say defensively.

I tried to understand and just thought he wasn't ready yet. We were
still months from his diagnosis when this was happening so each day
I imagined 'this would be the day' and when it didn't happen then,
'maybe tomorrow.' I'll come through the door, he will come running
and all will be right in the world. But that day never came.

Soon the evening downward spiral became a ritual. I would come
home, vie for little Em's attention and get none. I would sulk, lash out
or close up. Every night had a cumulative effect. Each night that I tried
to connect and didn't get any feedback, I got worse at handling it.

When the diagnosis came it all made sense, but it just put me into a deeper depression. Now I knew not to expect much, if anything when I came home. I became a defeatist as it got to where I didn't even try to get his attention. Furthermore, when I stepped through the door and hung my coat my wife would start to disgorge all she had read about our son's condition. It was like hearing Charlie Brown's teacher in the indiscernible "wha wa wha whawawa." My ears were bombarded with unfamiliar sounds and terms. "PDD, FAPE, IDEA, NOS, Early Intervention, ABA, Fragile X syndrome" and on and on and on... But the voice in my head was crystal clear. *I wonder if there's any wine left in the refrigerator.* And as I would pour myself a drink and watch my son stare at the wall or the spinning wheels of an up ended toy car, I thought *what a nightmare.*

I believe this is where most marriages disintegrate. In a way parents are told not to expect anything from their distant child, worse yet no one sits down and gives them any tools or mind set to help them bring their child to the here and now. The husband comes home and is immediately overwhelmed as he becomes lost in terms and theories that his wife starts burping out. Doggedly trying to save her child, she tries to share her latest discoveries and is in need of a spouse to talk to and confide in, but Dad quietly shuts down to his own thoughts as junior is cocooned in this invisible and seemingly impenetrable shell. He looks at his child staring in the distance, banging his head or overly focused on toy wheels and his heart sinks. *All I want is for my son to look me in the eyes, to acknowledge me when I come to the door. I hear all these strange terms and therapies, but what can be done now? Tell me how I can at least be greeted at the door. I've worked hard all my life and did all the right things before having a family. But this isn't what I signed up for. We did the amniocentesis to check for abnormalities, my wife ate well and took all her prenatal vitamins. We did all the right things God Damn it and still something still went wrong! How is it a drug addict can have a healthy child and we don't?*

There, I said what every parent thinks. I know this sounds selfish, politically incorrect and immature. Yes, it is all those things. But it's not a bad thing to let it out in the privacy of your home. And your wife is allowed to puke the same self indulgent misery now and again. It's not the best conversation to have, but it's what you feel and you have every right to let it see the light of day. At least now the two of you are talking. Yes it's commiserating, but guess what; now the pieces are on the table. Showing frustration and anger shows you care and though you're against the ropes, you're still in the game.

Wanting acknowledgement from your child isn't a bad thing and you're not a bad parent for wanting it.

Now put away the tears, cynicism and self pity and let's get down to what men do best, 'fixing things' or putting things together, without directions. Unfortunately and without question - in this case you will need direction, but from one father of an autistic child to the next I'll try to make this as user friendly as possible.

So let's start separating the pieces of your child's autism puzzle and focus on solving the things that will bring you the most joy when you see improvement. Having therapists work on tasks like matching colors or puzzle pieces is great but this book is designed specifically to address the things I think parents feel are most important, to build your child's emotion and bonding capabilities. So, moving forward, write down some of the bonding behaviors you wish to see and or other behaviors you wish to correct. You can call it a wish list or goals.

For instance:

Affection: Make it more specific, this will help narrow your behavior to elicit the particular behavior from your child. You want, 1.) kisses. 2.) hugs 3.) To sit in your lap without getting elbows or head-butts to the face. 4.) To turn and acknowledge your voice or the sound of his name.

Safety: Again, make it more specific. 1.) Stopping on command, keeping him from bolting. 2.) Stopping him from wandering. 3.) Dangers around water. This is a great concern and is addressed in the later chapter *Stop! For Safety's Sake*. 4.) To acknowledge the call of his name – you can see how some safety needs can overlap with affection.

What you will later realize is by working on just a few things on the wish list can have a profound effect on your child's all around behavior, not to mention your outlook.

CHAPTER 4

GET INVOLVED

NOW that you've started to wrap your mind around the fact that autism is malleable, now that you have written down or at least made a mental list of just a few key behaviors you want changed, you are now beginning the process of separating sections of the puzzle. Getting involved is the foundation to not running away. All the tactics and strategies grow from this one seed. If you're not involved with helping your child, there's little or no chance of the sticking around. And letting your wife do all the running around from one therapist to the next while you go to work is not good enough. Don't wait to come home at night to get all your information. This dynamic only allows you to sit back and critique your wife when she starts to go over "what happened at the doctor's office." It's too easy to say, "why didn't you ask this or do that?" Take time off, go to the therapist and IEP meetings with her and don't be afraid to ask questions. In most cases when I did go with Jen I found myself asking questions she would not otherwise ask or I was handling Emerson while Jen could focus on reviewing the assessments with the therapist. Going to these excruciatingly painful experiences resulted in an unplanned side effect. Jen and I were becoming a team. I'll admit she had to drag me to some of the appointments, but there wasn't one that I didn't feel that I didn't need to be there after it was over.

Becoming a team will help later when it comes to discussing your wish list with your wife. See if there's anything else different that's important to her to add to the list.

"Get Involved." I know, it sounds ominous and nonspecific. *How do I get involved in something that even the doctors don't understand? I can't even get my son to acknowledge my presence when I come home at night and nobody has any suggestions how to change it. How am I supposed to get involved?* These were my inner thoughts.

It is admittedly overwhelming, but wanting to change behaviors that motivate you is the place to begin. It fills your cup and may keep you from feeling completely bled dry. It gets you engaged and up close. Don't worry about feeling selfish about focusing on behaviors that would bring you joy. Just because you want him to blow out a candle or independently open presents on his third birthday because it would make you happy is not a bad thing. You're a parent first, a therapist second, but by addressing the things that are important to you, therapy is taking the front seat with parenting. We parents already have the hardest job out of anyone and we deserve some positive emotional outcomes for all we are going through. We should be focusing on developing emotional bonds while the therapist help with other tasks.

The number one reinforcement to developing emotional bonds – becoming relevant to your child! As I thought through the process of how I was going to go about connecting with Little Em I realized I first needed to become relevant in his eyes. Before I could expect anything from him I had to first establish myself as a person or at least an object of consequence. My voice, my presence and my needs all needed to be paid attention to if I was going be successful at developing any attention and eventually affection from him. I repeat these next sentences in the next chapter as I explain the root goal of the main therapies, but I want to make it clear where you will be starting in developing a relationship with your child. "What do you do when something is irrelevant in your life? You pass it over; you ignore it and stay in your world. Even if your child had all the other learning disabilities associated with autism but you were already relevant in their eyes, the therapy of training and teaching would be infinitely easier."

So, the million dollar question: *How do I get into my child's world and make myself and my needs significant enough for him to pay attention?*

In order to properly approach establishing a mutual loving relationship with your child we need to go into the current terminology, definitions and main therapies for autism. I know this starts out so dry, but trust me, by the end of the next chapter you will be onto a new hybrid therapy that is specifically designed to breach the emotional walls of autism. We will look at how and why the main therapies work on autistic children as well as where they fall short. It will also provide a better understanding of the structure that is needed to elicit affectionate behavior from your child.

Stay with me, you will soon be handed the first set of tools to be able to focus directly on developing affectionate parent/child family behavior and bonding.

CHAPTER 5

MAIN THERAPEUTIC STRATEGIES AND A NEW PRACTICAL APPLICATION TO DEVELOP EMOTIONAL BONDS KNOWN AS AABA.

I want to remain focused on our goal here. *Find me a way to start connecting with my child!* This is what I always asked myself after reading through the obtuse explanations of different therapies. But it's best to methodically review the most widely accepted therapies out there. It illustrates why specific tactics exercised later in the book actually work and how the new hybrid therapy specifically applies towards promoting emotional bonds and instilling affectionate behaviors from your child.

I'll wager when your child was first diagnosed a whole foreign vocabulary of abbreviations and terms were thrust upon you. Even when the terms were explained to me they still seemed abstract and gave me absolutely no ability in figuring out how to help bond with little Emerson in a practical sense. So I put together a list of definitions as well as the main styles of therapy and broke them down into laymen's terms. Being able to visualize what the terms truly represent is important in understanding how to help your child. At last it will also enable you to understand the reasoning behind the hybrid strategy I have developed to help incite 'proper' emotion and affection from an autistic child. However, if you're comfortable with the therapies of Integration, Prompting, Discrete Trials, Floor Time, ABA and Greenspan and their shortcomings, by all means go right to the paragraph **"What is the basic primary goal of both therapies?"** This will carry you nicely into the hybrid therapy towards the end of the chapter headed, **"Applied Affectionate Behavior or AABA."**

Integration: Integration is the effort of having your child integrated with normally developing children to learn proper social interaction. Social awkwardness or the inability to socialize is one of the keystone issues with autistic children. Autistic children don't have the tools to read other people's faces or social cues, the scene is utterly overwhelming and chaotic to them, they become upset and either shut down, have crying fits, bolt from the scene or any combination thereof. To help you better understand and have more compassion for your child's disturbing social behavior, it's been found in some MRI scans that the amygdala in the child's brain is overactive and doesn't allow the child to properly decipher facial expression. So don't be surprised when you try to take your child to a neighborhood birthday party and he or she behaves in an appalling manner. The problem becomes exacerbated because the parents start to isolate themselves further out of embarrassment, exhaustion and frustration. They don't know how to begin correcting the situation even though being around peers is one of the more important things the child needs.

I can't count the times I didn't recognize my son when he got into a new social situation. It's like he was possessed, acting out in thorny cantankerous ways. We looked like parents with no control over our child, and we were. Our son's behavior at the neighborhood birthday parties and gatherings was heartbreaking. He would bolt towards the woods, hide under the deck or in a corner of the garage, and cry and run away when we tried to get him to play with others in the sand box or swing set. We quickly realized we would have to take turns being his shadow. And more than once we both were driven to tears, utterly exhausted and emotionally beaten down after seeing how the other normal children played all day while the parents for the most part relaxed, laughed and drank.

But as exhausting as it is integration is so important. The sooner you can get your child acclimated to social surroundings the better because the older they get the harder it will be to teach, coax and coerce them into behaving properly in social settings, both emotionally and physically.

So how can I get my child to start playing with others or at least stay in the social setting? Start with a smaller group or just one other child. The biggest challenge may be finding another family with a child a similar age to work with you. But the idea is to tone down the chaotic scene of many children to only one or two others. We were lucky enough to have a couple understanding neighbors who are also great friends. I also have a niece who was about six years old at the time. Her maturity and understanding taught by my sister allowed my niece to keep trying to interact with my son. Next, try to place your child a setting you know he or she enjoys. For example, maybe your child likes to play around the spinning water sprinkler – (they love spinning objects, but here you may be able to integrate social play when they see other children running and jumping through it. There are other examples later in the book that will allow you to integrate play with other objects like ceiling fans). Perhaps they like a kiddy pool, or a swing set or a bouncer. The point is to get the other kids to play in a setting your child is already comfortable in. And with only one or two other children it's much less overwhelming.

You will most likely still have trouble getting your child to acknowledge the other playmates even though they may be trying to hug or talk to him. Here it may help to give the playmate a favorite treat, (popcorn, licorice, fishy crackers) and ask them to give it to your child. The hope and idea is to get your child to associate the playmate with a reward.

I will be honest and tell you the candy idea did not work for my son, though I liked the idea. What did work was toning down the environment to one or two playmates and repetitively placing my son back into the play setting every time he turned to run. I won't lie - its work and it's frustrating. At first it seemed like we made no

progress, but what you may find as we did, is each time we began a
little play session he did a little better than the last time in one area or
another. I remember when a particular playmate came over our house
out of the blue; Emerson smiled from ear to ear then ran around, not
quite knowing what to do with himself. The fact he was excited over a
visitor was a milestone. I started to see my son was in there, wanting to
come out and be the little boy he wanted to be. For me, getting him to
redirect or control his excitement was much less of a concern. Showing
positive emotion was the landmark.

Prompts: Prompting is the physical assistance to derive a wanted
behavior, (for example, placing your hand over theirs and helping
them open a door). This is a great tool in teaching your child a particular behavior, but it must be carefully monitored. For instance, we
were working getting our son to wave goodbye whenever I saw him
off. Normally he wouldn't even look at me as I repeated "bye bye" in
his face. It was heartbreaking and could easily be another nail in the
family coffin if I simply gave in and stopped trying. But one day out
of frustration I took his arm by the elbow and raised it up to make
him wave. He unexpectedly started to wave - or more like repeatedly
squeezing a tennis ball. Little did I know that I was using the tried and
true tactic of prompting. Raising his arm every time it was time to say
goodbye created consistency in trying to imprint the behavior, but we
were careful to first attempt to get him to do it on his own. If I did
physically have to hold his arm up it's important to let go as soon as
he began to wave to get him to do it more and more on his own. It's
very easy for the child and those trying to help him get dependant on
physical prompting and the sooner it's weaned off the better.

Discrete Trial: Or discrete trial training (DTT), Is a specific set
of exercises to test and teach a child's ability at a particular task. DTT
teaches skills and behaviors explicitly, where most children would pick
up these abilities naturally. For instance, let's use the trial to get your
child to stop running away upon command. You begin with holding
your child's hand and walking in a firm leading manner. You command
"Stop!" and come to halt, noticing the child would have kept walking

but only stopped at the physical prompt of you own body and hand stopping them short. This is the first 'discrete trial'. You begin again by saying "go!" and begin another trial again. As each trial progresses the child begins to respond by stopping easier with each command. Eventually you lessen your grip on the child's hand while continuing the trials. I am using this example since later in the book I go into great detail about this trial and how it is so important in developing parental relevance to the child and also helps address important safety issues with autistic children.

Rewards are extremely important, so it is imperative to find out what reward system really motivates your child.

Applied Behavior Analysis: Otherwise known as ABA, Applied Behavioral Analysis is the application of behavioral science. Now if that definition wasn't helpful in figuring out how to help your child, you're not alone. Many people associate Discrete Trials mentioned above with ABA and it is a key component, however, ABA is directed towards the changing of a person's behavior in the social setting. For instance, getting your child to respond to your commands to "Stop" in any environment meets this criterion. You are changing a behavior that has social significance, it is generalized (in other words the child is not just responding to this request in a single environment) and can eventually be used by anyone asking the child to stop. Discrete Trials are the specific exercises used to change the child's behavior. There are many variations of ABA based interventions out there: the UCLA model, Intensive Behavior Intervention (IBI), Applied Verbal Behavior (though similar to ABA, this is really a framework for the application of the science of Verbal Behavior), Discrete-Trial Training, Pivotal Response Training, and Natural Environment Training (NET). Each uses a unique system of instruction, but each is based on the science of ABA and the use of Discrete Trials.

Greenspan: Greenspan focuses much more on developing the child from an emotional level than developing rote tasks like ABA. Greenspan describes six milestones or stages of emotional progress that form an emotional and social developmental ladder. What is important is not so much the age at which a child masters each skill, but that each one is mastered in sequential order for each skill forms a foundation for the next. It is viewed as a ladder of sorts and supposedly the individual cannot successfully proceed to the next rung without mastering the prior level. The milestones go in the following order.

1.) Emotional self regulation and interest in the world. Developing the ability to not become over stimulated and staying engaged in the world around you. (I interpret this as the real world becoming relevant in the child's eyes, which is a cornerstone of this book.)

2.) Intimacy. The child understands warmth and affection are pleasant joyful experiences.

3.) Two way communication. Whether it is verbal or visual, developing two way communications is the premise to meaningful relationships.

4.) Complex Communication. The child's development of a vocabulary will make his requests and interactions more complex.

5.) Emotional Ideas.

Floor Time: Just as Discrete Trial is synonymous with ABA, Floor Time is synonymous with Greenspan's style of therapy. Instead of hard military like, repetitive trials that ABA professes, Floor Time takes the approach of getting down to the child's level, literally getting down on the floor and interacting with the child by playing with the toys or activities the child likes. Once the child accepts the caregiver's presence the relationship can begin to build on the six steps. The caregiver reads the child's expressions, instigates sharing and other interactions.

What is the basic primary goal of both therapies? To me, both Applied Behavior Analysis and Greenspan are attempting the same rudimentary goal up front. Whether it's setting up specific discrete trials to match colors or if it's getting down on the floor to instigate interactive play. The torn down basic goal is to get them out of their world and to make your voice, your wants and your face relevant to your child. What do you do when something is irrelevant in your life? You pass it over; you ignore it and stay in your world. Even if your child had all the other learning disabilities associated with autism but you were already relevant in their eyes, the therapy of training and teaching would be infinitely easier. ABA forces discrete exercises, specific tasks to teach them, but it makes your wants relevant which indirectly makes you relevant. Greenspan looks to directly make you relevant by getting into their world through interactive play and socialization.

Pros and cons of ABA and Greenspan: ABA is a regimented intensive therapy that breaks down therapeutic exercises into very specific tasks that can be measured for progression. If you look up experiments done by Dr. Lovaas you will see some very promising statistics. For instance, some members in the group that received the most therapy increased their IQ up to 33 points. It builds ability via rote robot like repetition. They simply keep working at an exercise until it's mastered like matching colors or shapes then build on that. However, critics say this therapy falls short when it comes to building affection and relationships.

Greenspan's approach towards first building a relationship in order to begin therapy falls on the other side of the spectrum. It seeks to build and develop relationships between the caregiver and the child. This directly addresses the social inadequacies autistic children typically have. However, this is a much softer approach to therapy and it can be extremely frustrating to attempt, especially for a parent who has little or no training. The parent or therapist attempts to go into the child's world by including themselves in the child's favorite activities. Progression is typically at a much slower pace because you are more dependant of how receptive the child is. At the end of the day, Greenspan's style makes it much more difficult to discern any improvement via increased ability in measurable task.

So as parent can I teach affection? And how can I do this without becoming completely frustrated. How can I possibly stay the course if I have no ability to bond or become relevant in my child's eyes? What specific exercises can I work on to help build a more normal family dynamic? Is this is your inner voice? I know these were the questions I was asking myself. Worse yet, other more unsettling thoughts would raise my heart rate. *How can I possibly potty train a child with no speech? How can I get him to not bolt or wander away? How can I get him to be comfortable being nose to nose with me or get him to look me in the eyes? In essence, how can I get him to be my son and not just an enclosed distant eyed stranger?*

What if somehow you could blend ABA to Greenspan and focus on tasks that instill affection and desire for bonding?

Applied Affectionate Behavior Analysis or AABA. As I term it, is the exercise of applying discrete trials for the sole purpose of teaching and inciting affectionate behavior in your child. I term them **Discrete Affectionate Trails or DAT's.** It subscribes to the importance of Greenspan's mantra, but enforces the patterns of a loving family social system though ritualistic and systematic behaviors. This doesn't just mean coming home, getting into your child's face and trying to kiss and hug them, but developing tactics and behaviors to get your child to first find you relevant and progressing towards hugs, kisses and general affection. Many criticize ABA for creating "little robots", that it doesn't teach emotion or the finer social interactions so many autistic children commonly lack. I'm sure some will criticize my blended hybrid style as well. That I may be teaching the child the "habit" of kissing or hugging, but they aren't truly feeling it. My answer to that is autistic children need to begin somewhere. The only way for them to realize a hug or a kiss actually 'feels good' is to not simply hug and kiss them, but to get them involved in the action or act of affection. Simply giving kisses allows them to passively remain in their world, but putting them through prompted physical and behavioral exercises of typical family behavior is designed to pull them from their world and participate. It may be rote and robotic at first, but I have seen amazing progress via the strategies laid out in the later chapters.

Just because an autistic child does not have the innate ability to know a hug feels good or they constantly put knees and elbows out because they're uncomfortable with close quarters doesn't mean you should enable it to continue or that they can't learn and eventually want affection.

Here is a prime example. After some time of putting Emerson through the paces illustrated later, we did get him to give us kisses upon request even though he was looking away as he did so. And I will be the first to admit he kissed me like a dead fish. It was rote. However, before working him through the exercises, just getting him comfortable with closing the distance between our faces was previously insurmountable. As the exercises took hold, he became increasingly comfortable will being physically closer and closer to us. He would even turn and I could get a glimpse of those beautiful eyes as he looked at me! It was a precious gift. An instance occurred where Little Em wanted a popsicle. Of course he went to the refrigerator on his own, but I was right there attempting to get him to verbally request it. He couldn't say the word, and it always broke my heart as I watched the words get lost behind his eyes. I kept repeating "Pop" with it next to my eyes as I tried to keep him engaged at attempting speech. But out of nowhere he suddenly gave me a kiss in an attempt to coax me to give him the popsicle. The cute interaction not only brought about some of the few happy tears I've ever shed, but this is an example of the type of small openings these "rote exercises" create. These little surprising incidents provide the toehold to help keep the family working together and build the affectionate interactions you so desire as a parent.

Greenspan's style of getting into your child's world is through interactive play, but to me, attempting to wiggle into your child's mind by simply getting down to his level and searching for ways to become relevant under their terms can be akin to going into the woods and befriending a pack of wolves. It takes an extraordinary person with an infinite amount of time, training and patience to be accepted into their world. This is not to say that Greenspan's ladder of connection and socialization isn't important. As a matter of fact it's imperative, but a main reason it hasn't been implemented more is because it's too frustrating, takes too long and doesn't have much in the way of proving progress because it's not set up with systematic exercises like ABA. Through AABA you create the opportunity and apply the ABA model toward creating and reinforcing behaviors that will later turn to natural affection.

The blended therapy of AABA focuses directly on the parent child relationship. Like Greenspan it must begin with a ladder of progression as well. But as shown in the next chapters, there are specific exercises to walk you through progression. To develop affectionate bonds you must begin with the very basics, which honestly is not very fun.

1. You must first become relevant in your child's eyes and ears. You can't possibly expect kisses and hugs or excitement when they see your face if your voice and presence are meaningless to them. Furthermore, getting in your child's face and saying "Dada?" Or "Mama?" is jumping way ahead. You also can't expect 'mama or dada' or other speech if you are meaningless in your child's eyes. For you to become relevant to them, they must understand that your voice, commands and wishes must be addressed. How do you accomplish that? By beginning with the rote exercise of "stop and go" illustrated in the next chapter. By first addressing the omnipotent safety issues you are also developing an ever so basic relationship with your child. It is a rote and rather non affectionate relationship, but you are establishing the most rudimentary requirement in the relationship – to become pertinent and present in their world.

2. Once your voice becomes significant a funny thing happens. When you speak your child then realizes he must pay attention. This reaction naturally begins to pull the child out of their world and into yours. He may not have the ability to like or dislike you or identify you as the parent at this juncture, however, now you have the ability to make other requests that he will be more likely to do. As a note, don't be surprised if

he is cantankerous towards the new exercises that force him to behave in the way you desire. It's a function of him not being happy about being forced to come out of his world and listen - and that's a good thing.

3. The physical and prompting rituals you set up about the family dynamic will eventually become part of his and your daily routine. Don't be surprised or disappointed that the motions your child goes through are mechanical at first. That he does them to simply appease the powers that be around him, but it does give parents comfort and a toe hold that they are making progress in developing emotion. Also, as I illustrated before with the popsicle incident, they can pleasantly surprise you down the road.

As you go through the daily rituals of family greeting, bedding down, stop and go, speech therapy is naturally associated with the actions. Most speech therapists will tell you to work on nouns, things or objects that the child desires instead of verbs. But as in the case of Little Emerson, his first word was "go!" because the word brought him lots of joy and enabled him to run. It was the result of setting up a structured training session of "stop and go". What started out as a regimented exercise to stop the bane of bolting had wonderful side effects. The structured exercise illustrated in the next chapter allowed me to take advantage of the one time I ever saw him smile, it taught counting, speech and began the ever so important interactive relationship between father and son.

Synopsis

Believe it or not some tools have already been placed in your hands. 1.) You have changed your mindset to take on autism. 2.) You've become determined to get involved instead of sitting on the sideline. 3.) Now you're armed with a new strategy, a hybrid therapy specifically designed to develop affection.

So let's begin the journey of first becoming relevant to your child and then apply Discrete Affectionate Trials to help bring your child to the here and now and weave the family fabric back together.

CHAPTER 6

STOP! FOR SAFETY'S SAKE.

ADDRESSING THE SAFETY ISSUES AND THE LEADING CAUSES OF ACCIDENTAL DEATH AMONG AUTISTIC CHILDREN, ALL WHILE TAKING THE FIRST STEP TOWARDS MAKING YOURSELF RELEVANT TO YOUR CHILD.

I'M starting with safety issues and tactics to change behavior since they are arguably the most important. In my view it is also the rudimentary starting point to becoming a person of significance to your child. The good part is you will be addressing two things at once. The bad is this will most likely not be the part that brings you the most joy. But the sooner you can provide a safe environment and gain control of dangerous behaviors the sooner the anxious knot in your chest can begin to unwind. Furthermore, as you go through the exercises I will illustrate how they will help with bonding, vocabulary, interactive play and discipline towards other inappropriate behavior further down the road.

Bolting and deaf eared wandering can be one of the more disappointing and dangerous behaviors of an autistic child. It's amazing how quickly things can degrade to chaos and panic with an autistic child, especially when you don't have any understanding of their condition or how to correct it. I'll illustrate some of Little Em's situation and then show how I corrected it. We have a small stream in the back of our property. In the low water month of August the small fish can be seen and caught easily. It's the perfect atmosphere for little boys to learn how to fish, make little dams, find crawfish and basically test the boundaries of our washing machine. But if he were to get back there by himself it was the perfect place to drown. Little did I know at the time how spot on our concern was as illustrated below. This event took place just before his diagnosis.

Emerson always wanted to go to the stream so I catered to this with every opportunity. He seemed happiest and there were glimmers of communication as I showed him how to toss rocks into the water. I remember one day trying to get one of the fish on a hook while he threw stones just a couple feet away. He was dressed the part in a cute little camouflage shirt with matching pants and hat. I was trying to get his attention to see the fish nibbling on the bait, but he was doing his own thing.

One fish took the bait. I yanked and it spit the hook. Hmmm. Another one hit the line, but missed that one too. Then I saw a big spotted trout wading in the deepest part of the pool observing the other fish with cat like indifference. (It was just over 5 inches.) *If I could only get him! Imagine the look on little 'Em's face!*

I eased the battered worm over in front of the trout's mouth. It bumped the trout's nose before he slightly turned away. *Maybe if I tease the line a little.* I jiggled the line and snap! He went for it.

"Oh my God! Emerson, look what I got!" I cheered as I looked up ready to put the pole in his hand.

He was nowhere in sight. (*Mistake #1, not paying attention 100% of the time.*)

"Emerson!" I panned the immediate surroundings. "Emerson!" He wasn't in any of his usual spots where he threw stones. I was in the only part of the stream deep enough to be a danger, but the road was only fifty feet from the other side of the stream and most of it was shallow enough for a two year old to walk right across.

Oh shit! I dropped the pole with the trout struggling on the end of the line. "Emerson!" A thousand horrible thoughts crushed my head.

The adrenaline made my heart thump like a sledge hammer against my breast plate as I kept scanning the woods for any movement. I was frozen, I didn't know where to begin and I was scared to abandon the one spot of water deep enough for him to drown. *Damn it! I only looked away for a few moments, maybe ten seconds. But how could I explain this to Jen or the police?*

It also hit me at the same time that I was looking for a twenty some pound toddler donned in full camouflage in mature forest greenery. (*Mistake #2.*)

"Emerson!" I started running down stream towards the thickest part of the woods.

I saw movement.

Little Em was wandering down a deer path ambivalent to my frantic calls. I purposefully called his name to see if there was a response, but he didn't turn, didn't look and didn't pause. This is nothing new to parents of autistic children and it was one of the key indicators for his later diagnosis, *but what can I do to correct this?* Catching my breath and holding back tears, I realized just how dangerous this trait was.

Jen came down after hearing my frantic calls and found me following just inches behind Emerson. "Is everything okay?" She asked. I noticed Emerson didn't have any reaction to his mother's voice or presence either.

I thought about lying, but I was so full of adrenalin that my mouth just let it go. "I lost him." She glared at me as I tried to explain myself. "It was for only a second. I got a fish on the line and when I looked up he was gone." She absently looked away with a sickened glare trying to fight back the tears. She knew I had done nothing wrong and this was just what we were dealing with.

She started to follow him with me. "Look at this," I said. I called out his name loudly only two or three feet from him. Yet he just kept wandering without looking back.

Both our hearts were breaking. "We can't dress him like this when he comes back here." I said. "From now on he has to have bright colors on." I scooped him up. Jen was tearing up and I wanted to distract her. "I have a fish on the end of the line," I said to her. "You want to see his reaction when he pulls it up?"

She wiped her tears and nodded.

After his initial diagnosis we had our first meeting with a group of therapists for early intervention. I brought up the safety concerns and they all nodded knowingly. I hadn't realized this is something very typical of autistic children. *Great, maybe they have some solid tactics to get this in line*, I thought to myself and asked what could be done to correct this.

"Well, if you can't put up a fence you can get caution tape and put it around a certain perimeter of your property. Walk him around it so he gets to know the border."

I felt like I hadn't got my point across. There was no way my son would respond to walking him around a yellow taped perimeter. "My son bolts from my hands, he doesn't respond to me at all. And if I had a fence, how is that going to help teach him to listen to me?"

"You just have to keep bringing him back within the borders every time he crosses and eventually he will understand. Repeating something ten or thirty times may be what it takes for a normal child to learn. You may have to repeat something five hundred or a thousand times before your child learns."

Okay, I thought to myself. "But how do we get his attention?" I asked. "What about the lack of eye contact? How do we develop a connection with our son so he can learn? I mean if he's not looking at me or hearing my voice, how is he going to absorb anything I'm repeating?"

"That's the trick," she explained. "If they were mentally here, it wouldn't be so hard. You have to be extremely patient and just keep trying."

"But simply repeating myself doesn't bring him out of his other-world. If my sounds are meaningless and I don't have his attention, then all the repeating in the world won't matter." *Is this all the behavioral training I get to pull my son out of this? Aren't there certain 'how to' exercises that can be given to us?* Not to keep reiterating myself, but this is why I felt so driven to write this book.

She assured me that it may seem I was wasting my time repeating myself, but one day it would all start to "click".

I'm sorry, but simply repeating myself until I was blue in the face wasn't good enough for me. So I asked the therapist again, "how would repeating myself before an indifferent, mentally deaf child who wouldn't look me in the eye get anything accomplished?"

I think she wondered if I had the learning disability. "You just have to keep repeating yourself." She said as her eyes rounded with frustration.

"How can I establish property boundaries when he doesn't even respond to his name or my voice?"

"You may want to consider swimming lessons." It was obvious she was simply redirecting me for lack of a better answer to my question (by the way this is a classic tactic to stop a child from an unwanted behavior). She continued, "Exposure to the elements, getting hit by vehicles and drowning are the leading causes of death with autistic children."

I will go more into the importance of swim lessons next, but let's stick to addressing the deaf run and wandering with some more sophisticated strategy and focus other than just repeating yourself. Since I wasn't getting any help I knew I had to come up with something more than just showing him boundaries.

It took me about six months of him bolting in parking lots and other scary situations before I pulled out my final card. In my opinion, walking perimeters while holding your child's hand as the therapist suggested won't typically make you or your commands important enough to an autistic child for them to learn. You must first establish the fact that you must be listened to. As with Emerson a much more rote, basic tactic had to be exercised.

I decided to try something that I internally had a problem with at first, but as I educated myself on ABA, I let my reservations go for the hope of progress. Little did I know that this rote reinforcement would not only mark the beginning of developing safety parameters, but it would set the foundation for speech, counting and most importantly - a father son relationship.

Ten years earlier I bought a cute little fur ball from a puppy mill. A Keeshond (pronounced Keese Hound) I named Mugsey. He chewed my furniture, destroyed my carpets and worst of all, he would bolt in a deaf run when we got outside. After eight weeks of poop, piss and general destruction I was ready to give him away, but as a last resort I hired a dog trainer. When he arrived I immediately noticed how the man took control of the situation. He was consistent and stern. He marched my dog around on a taught leash first putting him through the paces of stop and go. Soon he had me marching up and down the lawn and barking out commands for me to exact in military fashion.

I soon realized he wasn't training the dog; he was training me, changing my behavior by making my wishes perfectly clear in a rote military consistent fashion. He was doing something else as well. He was forcing my wishes to be of consequence to my dog. The animal that once was deaf to my commands was very suddenly falling in line and best yet, Mugsey began looking up at me for direction. Soon other behaviors such as going potty outside and not chewing began to sink in – all because my voice and my commands became significant. When I thought back to that time I realized that my puppy ignored me in the same way my son did.

So, I decided not to view the stream and woods behind our house as a hazard, but as an opportunity instead. Though Emerson wouldn't vocalize it, he loved the stream, and when we let him out the back door he would bolt for it. We would inevitably chase him in a deaf run all the way to the stream calling for him to slow down the whole way. It wouldn't matter how much we screamed or called his name to stop, he would simply keep running. At first this was extremely upsetting. But I remember running alongside him one day and looking over. For the first time I saw his face lit up in a beautiful open mouthed smile and it was also the first time I saw a lucid look in his eyes as we ran towards the stream.

This is where I started. Instead of just letting him run out the back, I kept a firm grip on him. Once outside I got down on my knees in front of his face. Of course he stared through me towards the stream. "Do you want to GO?" No response, but that was okay, I wasn't expecting one. So I stood, held his hand firmly and said "go" as I proceeded to walk towards the stream in a slow controlled manner. He pulled hard, tried to let go, but I firmly pulled him in and said "stop!" as I physically stopped as well. He fought me and he cried, but that meant he was fighting my wishes. We were combating whose will was going to be more relevant and it was going to be mine. Another thing any child will do but especially autistic children is flopping from your grip or arms to get away. This would be particularly disturbing with Emerson since he would develop that blank stare. I will illustrate later in this chapter how important it is to nip this behavior immediately. A stern "No" or "Stop" with an overwhelming jolt to his feet should be implemented. Letting your child pour through your hands as they flop to the ground will only reinforce them to use this behavior again and again. I soon realized I had to get Jen on the same page as Emerson figured out he could get away with this more with her than he could me.

Okay, back to the rote exercises. We went through controlled stop and go paces until he calmed down and began to follow my commands. It was amazing how quickly he began to fall in line. Before letting him bolt off for the stream, I crouched down in front of him again and counted with my fingers in his face. "One, two, three….. Go!" I then left him in the dust looking back as I ran towards the stream. He immediately caught on and ran with me towards the stream. We were both running and laughing. I was laughing because I was no longer chasing him down from a deaf run. For the first time he listened to my stop and go commands and we were now running together with the precious look of joy on his face.

I took the opportunity to take his hand and bring him to a quick stop with my other hand in front of his face as sign language for the command. He stopped. He didn't melt down, he didn't look at me either, but he did point towards the stream! Now I was getting communication. "Do you want to go?" I said right in his face. I stood, said go and walked in a controlled manner towards the stream. Then "Stop!" with the palm out in front of his face and bent down before him again. "One, two three…go!" and I started running before him. He burst into little squeals and began running again.

What a joy going to the stream became compared to the day before. We were now connecting.

Many people compare much of ABA discrete trails like teaching 'Pavlov's dog'. Yes it may seem demeaning and undignified of training an autistic child. But the sooner we get past ourselves here and focus on what's best for the child, the sooner you and your child can progress past this rote level of instruction. The best part is you will be able to see discernable changes in behavior which will considerably lower your frustration level and empower you as a parent to feel more in control of the situation. At first this seems like only a disciplinary exercise, but adding the little count and run make it an interactive fun experience for both. Also keeping myself in front of him as he ran – between him and the place he wanted to go kept me in his sights. I was now becoming part of his world. I could watch the open mouthed joy as he ran and I began to get lucid glimpses from those beautiful eyes of his. These are the little gifts the rote exercises can give in return.

Before trying this at home, make sure you are heading for something the child is eager to get to like a swing set, a sand box or even a favorite toy or candy off in the distance. It can even be something you may have previously tried to prevent him from running to. I've seen kids who like to watch automatic doors open and close and will bolt to go and repetitively open and close them. The parent or care giver simply pulls him from the door after catching up and removes him back to the task he bolted from. I say use this type of bane to your advantage. This is a perfect opportunity to make a bad habit an opportunity to develop relevance and connection. Set up a controlled go and stop walk towards the door. Point and make him point for what he wants. Count to three then beat him to the door so now you are included in the bolt for the door. Let him open and close it then move on to another task. Better yet, if he wants to keep playing with the door, set up the exercise from a distance again. You will be reinforcing communication, fun and your relationship.

I continued this exercise in the house, walking him by the hand saying the word "go" and "stop" in a very firm manner. He didn't look up at me and had to be physically stopped by the pull of my hand. Again and again I firmly walked him about the house commanding "go" then "stop," constantly starting up then coming to an abrupt halt. I tried to make sure it was as random as possible so he could not pick up on any pattern as well. I could tell Jen wasn't exactly comfortable with my "dog training" tactic but I was too worried about his safety.

The results were nothing short of amazing. After months of frustration and zero improvement, my changed behavior caused a dramatic change in his behavior. When I previously did what the therapist suggested and walk him about the perimeter of our property, I could see nothing was getting through. I realized that before he could grasp the advanced concept of property boundaries, he would first have to realize this big stranger next to him had to be listened to.

Within a few weeks of the stop and go exercise he did something for the first time after I brought him to another abrupt halt. I had hardly been paying attention myself as I had gone through the exercise countless times, but I suddenly realized he was looking up at me waiting for my command to go! What a breakthrough.

Not only was he following my commands. But my voice was becoming pertinent to his little ears. I was getting his attention! In my experience the obtuse and blunt tool of, "be repetitive," should not be the only tool. It needs to be enforced with an action that is required of your child. To really be effective the verbal command has to be accompanied by a controlled environment and reinforced with physical prompting. If they're not involved in the action, they are still insulated in their world and you will have a much harder time of experiencing any improvement.

As a therapy Jen and I made a point to take Emerson for a walk on a daily basis. At opportune times I would make us stop. I then made a point to get down in front of him and count before excitedly shouting "go!" His eyes would light up and off we went. Here again I was using his habit of bolting away as a tool to work in structured cooperative play. Did he not always comply and run away instead of with me? Did he fight me off when I tried to rein him in from a neighbor's yard? Absolutely. But he did understand as I bent down that he was about to be freed and for those fleeting moments I had his attention – his eyes were on me and an anxious smile curled his lips.

Walking with your child as a therapy may sound inane and non communicative, but there is so much opportunity to improve interactive play and socialization if you apply these type of exercises along the way.

By the third week I was having spotty success at commanding him to stop at a distance! We were in the back woods and he was about twenty feet away. I yelled "Stop!" and he froze. I was shocked. I ran up and looked over his shoulder to his face and there he was, smiling and waiting for me to tell him it was okay to go. It was becoming a game to him. The tactic couldn't have worked out more perfectly. My biggest regret was not implementing this until he was over two and a half years old.

Some may criticize me for comparing the development of my son to the training of my dog. But the fact is the sound of my voice now had meaning. I was now a person of consequence and within the span of just a few weeks of changing my behavior he looked up to my eyes for direction. For my autistic child to look in my face for direction was a monumental step forward. Not to mention it's a behavior that helped me bond with him.

As with most ABA training, the major criticism of using rote; mechanical repetition does little if anything to develop proper emotion and socialization, but this tactic first employed out of desperate need for safety had very beneficial side effects. As you will see in later chapters, training behaviors in affection exercised in a consistent military like fashion can create the emotional foundation many autistic children are lacking. The emotion will come; they will learn to understand that a hug and a kiss feel intrinsically good. They simply need to be put through systematic participatory exercises of affection.

As I mentioned before, others argue this sort of teaching is insulting and equated to 'Pavlov's dog', but as is with my son, what started out as a Pavlov's dog eventually progressed into eye contact and facial feedback. If I had never tried it I guarantee I would not have experienced the eye contact or smiles.

I got more than I could have hoped for from this one behavioral tactic. What started out as a desperate attempt to address safety issues blossomed into a rewarding connection. And God forbid if he ever starts running head long into danger, perhaps the command to "stop!" will not be ignored and save his life.

Case in point. At just over three and a half years old, Emerson did love to ride with me on the lawn tractor. He was at the point of being able to stick around while I would spread mulch on the landscaping. It was a tentative balance because after a few minutes he would typically start to wander off, but once I called him to come back and started the tractor he would come running back all excited to ride. Well, in the middle of spreading mulch a double axel dump truck entered the neighborhood. It was only traveling maybe ten miles an hour, but he was obviously carrying a heavy load. Emerson bolted in a direct intercept for the truck at the road. "Stop!" I commanded over the loud diesel engine. He halted in his tracks. I approached in a calm walk and bent down to his face. "Thank you!" I said with a big smile.

This exercise helped alleviate another more completely frustrating situation that any parent has. My voice now had meaning and had become an integral part of his world. I was no longer fruitlessly repeating myself and getting nowhere. Of course there are times I am completely ignored. Sometimes ignoring your parents is just part of what a three year old does.

SWIM LESSONS

Okay, back to the swim lessons the therapist suggested earlier. How important is daddy and swim lessons? If you're not there to give swimming lessons it just increases the chances of him becoming a tragic statistic. Autistic children are particularly attracted to water. Their lack of fear, natural silence and propensity to wander makes for a potentially lethal combination. Even if you're separated from your spouse and you have abandoned your responsibility at every other level, there are at least two things you should do as a daddy. Take your child for swim lessons and attend the IEP meetings.

Before little Em was diagnosed in early summer we took him to a friend's pool for a first time swim. We got him a little life jacket and were excited yet a bit anxious about his first dip into a real pool. It became quickly apparent he had no fear. Worse yet he wouldn't jump in, he would simply step off the copping. No loud splash to signal a child falling in the pool, just a quiet little 'bloop' and he would sink if it wasn't for the life jacket.

He had a blast in the pool as I kept hold, but I was very scared for his welfare the entire time. I remember my wife and I both realizing we would have to take turns shadowing him once he was out of the pool. There was no way we could trust ourselves to sit with the other adults, drink wine and laugh and think we could properly monitor him. We had to tag team him. We took turns eating and relaxing while the other literally shadowed our son. I can't imagine being a single parent in situations like this. They would have to simply pack up a go home after the swim.

So we set up swimming lessons. I remember hearing that father's tend to do better with swim lessons. They're stronger and the children respond better to dad's firm hands. I can't say there's any proof to this theory, but it's nice to hear there's something that father's supposedly excel at.

At two and a half years of age we signed Emerson up for his first swim lessons at the YMCA. I highly recommend this facility. They have locker room facilities set up for adult men and women and separate locker rooms for parents and children under seven. When signing him up for Daddy and Tot swim lessons we mentioned his condition and they simply said 'this should be very good for him.' No hesitation, no stigma.

Ironically we failed to realize his first lesson was within a couple days of my scheduled vasectomy and the doctor advised against being submersed in pool water so soon. We had painfully decided for no more children after our son's diagnosis. I was forty three at the time and with evidence that autism is tied to older men and other possible genetic factors, I was not willing to risk bringing another child into this world with this condition or worse.

Now, after sitting on the side lines watching my wife try to corral my over stimulated son I now have proof that men are better at dealing with autistic children in the water. As the other infants trustingly let their parents glide them along the surface Little Em pushed away, kicked and grunted in strange unnerving ways. Jen had to contend with a number of upper bathing suit malfunctions from my son's clawing and yes, we got the raised eyebrows from the other parents. It's hard still, but I'm getting better at just laying it out on the table. "He's autistic." There's not much more explanation necessary, they usually nod apologetically and turn away, maybe a little embarrassed over their judgmental glare.

Don't get me wrong, Emerson was having a great time, but it was on his own terms. There was no semblance of listening to the teacher in the center of the group. He over-climbed on Jen's face and kicked and screamed in unnerving ways through the entire session. Jen looked to be on the brink of tears a couple times. I couldn't tell if it was from embarrassment, frustration or exhaustion. I'm sure it was all of the above.

On the way home I looked over to her beleaguered eyes and said. "It was like watching Mini-me attack you with his newfound karate skills downloaded from The Matrix." We both got a laugh out of it. Sometimes I've got to make light of a situation to see my way through.

Autistic children, especially the ones that get over stimulated or frustrated easily have an innate knack at head butting under the chin, throwing a knee into a breast or stomping on daddy's crotch. It's definitely dad's job to be in the pool. Our strength and stern demeanor not only helps control their over stimulation it also helps calm and bring them emotionally down to a better place.

I hosted the swim lessons from that point on. I'll admit my son was so cantankerous sometimes we would call the lesson short and leave early. I was frustrated and disappointed a number of times. One positive constant, however, was the rare smile on his face every time he saw that pool. It was a tricky balance between letting him paddle on his own and trying to get him to participate in the group exercises. Soon I learned to work within the outer perimeter of the group. The irony was that he was the quickest learner of independent swimming of the bunch. By the end of the first six weeks, he was naturally swimming horizontally. The teacher noticed first, remarking that most children try to swim standing up, like they're running under water and it usually takes years for many children to learn to put their body horizontal. I was bruised, battered and exhausted, but her compliment made all the pain of that day go away.

There were some fun moments too. When trying to teach him to blow bubbles into the water I playfully streamed a mouthful of water at him just to get his attention as he was staring off to the other side of the pool. Well he didn't learn to blow bubbles, but he did learn to spit water back at daddy. I didn't care, he thought it was the funniest thing in the world, and I was finally getting some banter and interaction from my son, even if it was at the chagrin of the other parents watching.

Another important factor in the lessons was to have Jen there. By the end of the lessons I would be utterly worn out. The idea of trying to change myself and my son after the swim would have proven extremely difficult and frustrating. When the lessons were over, Jen would change him out while I licked my wounds and coughed out the water I swallowed in the other locker room. Thank God.

The one mistake was that we constantly kept him in a full life jacket because he was so good at shucking off my hold. I didn't expect Emerson to become such an independent little paddler at thirty months, but by the end of his first six weeks of lessons he could stroke his way across the width of a pool (with the jacket on of course). Though the life jacket immensely helped me keep him above water when he initially pushed and kicked away from me, I soon realized he thought he could always float in water and I had inadvertently undermined my original reason for the lessons. Water was even more dangerous now. Fortunately we had access to a neighbor's pool to illustrate how a life jacket kept him afloat. I tried to correct this by letting him jump in without the life jacket. Of course I was right there in the water. After retrieving him from a few self inflicted dunkings I put the jacket on and he happily swam around. I then brought him to the ladder and removed the jacket and let him try to swim again. Soon he was reaching for the jacket before going to the edge of the pool. But a couple weeks later and he was ready to jump in without the jacket. This illustrates the poignant yet all too common trait of regression in autistic children. To this day we're still working on getting him to understand the need for a life jacket. I'm simply illustrating where I went wrong so you can try to avoid the same mistake.

As frustrating and tiring as swim lessons may be, it involved everyone. It kept interaction within the whole family and helped strengthen the fabric of marriage. However, if just Jen or I went to the lessons alone and tried to work with Emerson I can bet it would build animosity instead.

ANOTHER UPDATE ON THE STOP AND GO PROCEDURE:

I could argue to put this update in the chapter regarding temper tantrums and curving other behavior, but I figured since I specifically used the stop and go trial to correct unwanted behavior I thought it would help you see the importance of instilling this behavioral relationship with your child.

Again, just past the age of three and a half I spent the day at Emerson's school. I wanted to sit in on the discrete trials so I could mirror them at home. The stop and go trials I instituted had been in place for about one year and I had recently built upon them. I was trying to get him to stand in place even while at a distance from me. I would open my hand up to his face in the universal stop sign to stay where he was as I backed away. This took some doing since he kept trying to walk with me. I finally put him at the top of a short set of stairs and the change in level helped keep him there as I taught him to stay in place. I was attempting to instill control at a distance while using sign language. I came to realize that while in public many people will turn and glare when I bark my orders. At this age I was having success at getting him to stop on command, but of course it depended on how far away I was.

An interesting thing happened as I worked him through this. By now I had already implemented all of the other exercises you will read in the next chapters so I had instilled some proper affectionate behaviors. When I bent down and finally gave the word for him to come to me he started opening his arms and saying "ug". It was very quiet and I hadn't realized he was trying to say the word hug! Here I was caught up in building on relevancy and control at a distance and he was teaching me to stay affectionate and have fun! This from a child who didn't want to be touched, couldn't tolerate close nose to nose contact, whose eyes rolled white in his head if I tried to make him look at me and was utterly deaf and blind to my presence only a year and a half ago. Again, I'm simply trying to illustrate the little gifts these exercises can surprise you with.

So, I went to the school to observe. During circle time the individual teachers sat with the students in their laps. To my dismay Emerson flopped and writhed as the teacher kept trying to pick him up and sit him proper in her lap, but he kept pouring through her arms like sand. "He doesn't like circle time very much." She said as she kept trying to get him in her lap. I was appalled and upset. Emerson seemed completely disconnected with zero cognition and utter ambivalence that he was disturbing the entire group. This flopping behavior had not been tolerated from day one and completely curbed for over a year and a half in our household, or so I thought. I had a knee jerk reaction and didn't ask for permission to correct him. I bent down disturbing the circle time further and with a grinding voice as I got in his face, "Emerson stop!" I commanded with my palm open. "Up up!" I said as I motioned with my hand again. "Right now!" In an instant he sat up in the teacher's lap and the lucidity returned to his eyes. It was like his attention and awareness returned to the here and now and he became the little boy I knew once again. The teachers looked at me some-what shocked at my stern demeanor, but then raised their eyebrows in approval as they saw Emerson's cognition return to the room.

A similar thing happened later that morning in the school gym. The kids were lining up, each one with a teacher behind them, setting up to run to the far wall. Everyone seemed to be aware and anxious of the coming run, everyone but Emerson. He was flopping on the ground, resisting the teachers hold and sifting his limbs through her hands once again. The kids all ran to the far wall as Emerson was left behind flopping on the ground. This was utterly disturbing to me as Emerson looked to be the most severely handicapped and unaware of his surroundings. Here he was missing out on doing something I know he enjoyed while completely frustrating his teachers.

This time I asked if I could intervene and was obliged. I approached as everyone was preparing to run again. Once again, the sound of my voice and firm grip brought him out of his disturbing grunting struggle and right to attention. "Emerson. Stop!" I got down to his level and close to his face, "do you want to go? Do you want to run?" His eyes were suddenly lucid and a smile began to curl as I counted down just as I do whenever we go for walks to the stream. At the word 'go' the teacher and Emerson made for the wall in a giggly run. I headed back to the sideline to discuss my tactic when Emerson bolted from the teacher by the wall. I stepped out and intercepted his path with my palm out and a firm "Stop!" He stopped on a dime. I said, "thank you for stopping, now go back." And I pointed toward the teacher by the wall. He walked back to his place with the teacher.

The head teacher was shocked and wanted to know how long it took for me to develop that sort of verbal and gesture control. I let her know it was a building process, but at this point he would most likely take to following them within minutes.

At the end of the day I was very upset for not knowing his behavior of flopping and resisting was that bad, but it also reinforced that that my tactics were on the right path. For me, this was a clear example of Emerson's great change in behavior between someone who was of little consequence and relevance verses me whose voice and presence by now was of great relevance and consequence to him.

I'm not hinting that the teachers were not doing their job well, but I do believe that in many ways they are walking on egg shells and are at times hamstrung when it comes to the balance of discipline. When we discussed his inappropriate behavior the therapist are all given the same plan of action. To pick him up and physically prompt him through the task at hand. If he is still not complying, they run compliance trials until he begins responding to their instruction. Once he complies then reassess his reinforcements, (what rewards he is willing to work for).

This is a great methodical approach to changing inappropriate behavior, but whatever happened to good old fashioned intolerance to inappropriate behavior. This politically correct roundabout way to correct behavior fails to set boundaries for inappropriate behavior. I think in many instances these children are smarter than we give them credit. Here I observed my son behaving as if it were impossible to get through to him. He flopped, grunted and stared distantly in disturbing fashion. But once he heard my voice and realized there was no getting away with this behavior his lucidity came back into the room.

I wondered where his progression would be if I had never instituted these Discrete Affectionate Trails in the first place. I imagine he would have been even deeper in his world grunting, fighting and flopping. Autistic children work best with specific set boundaries and that goes for setting specific parameters for inappropriate behavior as well. This subject falls partially in the Enabling chapter later in the book, but autistic children will push boundaries just like any other normally developing child. But just because they're autistic doesn't mean they should be given more leeway for bad behavior. As a matter of fact it has to be addressed and nipped with more vigilance because the longer it goes on the harder it's going to be to correct. I can't imagine trying to curb a seven year old from bolting and flopping.

I requested to spend the day again at the school to put the same stop and go exercises and hand gestures in place. As for the flopping I requested they immediately and firmly scoop him up from the floor, this usually would 'wake him up' to the fact it will not be tolerated. If he keeps up he is to be immediately and firmly removed from the group and disciplined, (told to "stop" and possibly put in time out). They were not comfortable with some of this, arguing that it would disrupt the class, but I wondered which was worse – my son flopping on the ground, reinforcing to everyone else what could be tolerated or swift corrective discipline.

As a result of our collaboration Little Em is spending less time flopping on the floor and more participating in social exercises which is making full use of the therapy.

Synopsis
Safety measures

1) Train him to listen to your command of 'stop' or 'go.' Hold your child by the hand and walk him around the house stopping and starting at random times to the words stop and go. You may want to start indoors in a familiar area and then move to outdoors. Autistic children find it harder to focus in open spaces, but this is where there is usually the most danger so this is also the most important place to learn. Try to get

them to run while holding your hand then halt to quick stops. This will help them learn to obey in the future when they are most excited and least likely to listen, (like in a parking lot). Always get them in the habit of stopping at a curb. This is to imprint the process of stopping at the sight of any curb. Ask the daycare teachers or any relative who watches over to do the same thing when taking him to and from the play ground, bathroom, etc. Randomly commanding him to stop and go while holding their hand will make your voice relevant to your child and will hopefully draw them to eventually look up to you for direction. The fundamentals for two way communication are being constructed. When it seems they are listening, let go of their hand and continue the exercise. First at only a few feet then further and further away. Getting your child to stop bolting with a command may one day save his life. Later, after some of the other affectionate trials have taken hold, you can begin the exercise of getting them to follow hand signals of stop and go. This may be of particular use in public and will hopefully allow you to not have to use a stern voice so much.

2) As painful as it may be it's prudent to inform your neighbors of wandering habits. Let them know how to approach your child if there are any sensory issues. If the neighbor doesn't know your child has a wandering problem, they may not do anything if they see them alone in their own back yard.

3) Get your child swim lessons. Autistic children are particularly attracted to ponds, streams and pools. Drowning is one of the leading causes of death among autistic individuals. I don't believe simply keeping them away from water is the solution. They will be exposed to it eventually and it's best if you're there to oversee it. It may also turn out to be a rewarding activity in which you can see your child progress. The circumstance forces the child to depend and interact with you. It can have a profound effect on their internal dynamic – in other words, there will be times in which they will hold to you for safety in

the water which forces open child bonding to parents. It's best to do this as early as possible because trying to handle an over stimulated two or three year old is hard yet doable. Trying to handle and over stimulated six year old may be impossible.

4) Know your child's favorite spots. If he goes missing, know the first places to go and look for him.

5) If there's a propensity to wander place eye hooks on doors high up or other child safety door handles to all bathrooms, laundry room and exits to the house.

6) If your child is wanderer, lock him in his bedroom at night. Keep a monitor in the room for any disturbance.

7) Place an ID tag on their shoe with a name address and phone numbers. If there's room, write on the opposite side write the child's name and 'autistic.' Having an identification in the shoe helps insure they won't rip it off themselves.

8) There are a number of personal tracking devices that can be bought. They can monitor and track a child who may have wandered.

9) Make the daily walks a family habit and most importantly make them interactive and fun. Get in front of your child and count off before yelling "go!" This blends the discrete trial of ABA and the social connection of Greenspan. You will be able to see progression in his ability to listen to your commands while you are interacting and instigating play activities.

Well done. With the first exercise of 'stop and go', you are now beginning to create the foundation of becoming significant to your child. You have reached in and forced them to start looking outside their world and into your eyes. The following chapters will build upon this so your world and his will become more and more as one.

CHAPTER 7

COMING HOME AND GETTING HUGS. ENFORCING AFFECTION WITH ALL DUE MILITARY STRATEGY AND PRECISION.

A S you read in the previous chapter, getting your child to behave and respond in the fashion you want will require more than simply repeating things in his face or leading him around saying some words that have no physical action or behavior required from your child, (like walking him along a yellow taped property border line.) *So, how can I receive affection or greetings at the door at the end of the day?* Like the rote physical prompting exercised in the previous chapter, this can also be applied towards the family interactions of greetings, hugs and kisses.

As I was painfully immersed into the world of autism, I found out even the most rudimentary behavior has to be taught to some autistic children, so many of the small behaviors that make us human don't come naturally to these kids. But it's worse than simply working with a clean slate. You also must break through the emotional cocoon and meltdowns and then try to teach normal acceptable social skills. Quite a feat.

Emerson didn't have the proper emotional reaction when I came home at the end of the day. Indifference is a typical yet extremely disappointing trait of many autistic children. This unresponsiveness can cause some of the greatest amount of distress and grief to the parents. I know it did for me. As a father who dreamed of hugs and kisses when coming home, the indifference to my face and voice was gut-wrenching.

"Emerson!" I would say from behind the mud room door. "Daddy's home!" My wife would cry out excitedly every night, but when the door opened I got nothing. "Daddy's home, daddy's home!" Still I tried to get something as I approached the highchair in which he was eating his dinner. "Hi Emerson!" I would say with a clown's smile and animation.

Most nights he wouldn't even look up at me. I could scream his name, jump up and down and burp jelly beans, yet I was treated like an unseen ghost. Sometimes I said his name so loud he should have winced, but it wouldn't even induce a glance.

This is commonly where the downward spiral of marital dissolution and disconnection really begins to gain speed and I bet this is where most dads get lost. This is also where the frail male ego is so easily shattered. Again, as men we've been secretly waiting for our infants to become toddlers, to connect with them as little people. *I'm getting no feed back at all so what's the point of all this sacrifice? Why do I bother? I can't even get my son to look at me and he has no clue and could care less who I am. It's been two years since he was born and he still hasn't said a word, let alone 'dada."*

I now knew what it felt like to be an empty vessel. It was like I was losing blood, my son's indifference draining me of all hope for any semblance of family. Sometimes I felt like the family was already dead, so what's the difference if I left?

These were the voices in my head when I came home to this scenario and when I asked, other Dads agreed under their breath as they looked around to make sure no one else was listening. This is where we lose control, realize "we can't fix it" and begin our emotional tailspin.

Soon each night was like the last. The ritual of tossing my keys to the counter and furiously stomping around after failing to get

Emerson's attention was like a nightmarish Groundhogs Day. Now Jen had two dysfunctional children on her hands. As I began my nightly huff, Jen would typically defend him once again and an argument would ensue. Even though we had yet to get the diagnosis, (Emerson was nearly two) I realize now, looking back that our marriage was already separating at the seams.

Then one night as I stared at the back of Little Em's head after he refused to turn to greet me once again, something came over me. "That's it, we're going military," I said. Jen looked at me with worried eyes as I continued. "We are going to enforce affection upon him with all due military strategy and precision." I explained further. "Every night I'm going to call you on my cell phone so you can get him ready." Jen still seemed worried as I listed my demands. "I want the television off and I want him out of his high chair with no food in his mouth or bottle in his hands. I will then knock on the door and call his name. I want you to call out all excited and make him walk to the door." I had to make sure Little Em would be going through the motions as I made myself clear. "Don't carry him, he must walk to the door. If he melts down pick him up and make him walk again."

Damn it, I was going to get the greeting I wanted, even if I had to force it.

This was about a month before his diagnosis, so he was about 22 months old. I didn't realize it at the time, but I was setting up a therapy session of Discrete Trial – classic ABA, but with a twist. This was a Discrete Trial to imprint proper affectionate behavior and emotion. I also didn't know at the time that autistic children do best with structure. Structured environment, structured times and structured behavior is a proven successful strategy of teaching children with autism. ABA as I explained earlier relies on this; structured environment, movement and task. We were also prompting him. By getting rid of all distractions (food, bottle, television) and physically leading him to the door, taking his hand and helping him use the door knob, putting him through the motions of being there and giving me a hug were therapeutic ABA strategies.

But what about emotion? I wanted my son to love me! I just wanted a smile on his face. As mentioned before with the rote structure of leading my son through the stop and go exercises, this is one of the greatest critiques of ABA. That rote, mechanical, one-on-one discrete trial therapy doesn't build the necessary social skills or emotion. But this AABA exercise structured in an ABA fashion was for the sole purpose of not only illustrating, but also enforcing affectionate behavior. I know the term sounds harsh, "enforcing affectionate behavior", but what you're really forcing here is for children to come out of their world and to participate in yours. You're not just raining down hugs and kisses upon them, you're making them become part of the exercise itself.

This is where you as a father come in and the cold Discrete Trials of a therapist leave off. Yes, the therapists give your child rewards like hugs or candy for wanted behavior, but no one else is his father and no one else can instill that awe or safety a dad can instill in his child's heart.

This is where you can begin to teach affection and proper emotion.

Just opening the door at night and saying "Here I am," gives the child every opportunity to ignore you and it gives you every opportunity to pout and give up. You must regroup and approach this as an exercise to be executed with consistent military precision.

At first, I called Jen from the garage so she could prepare Emerson's environment, but later came to find it was not enough time for him to calm down after being pulled from his comfortable zone. Food abruptly taken out of his hand, pulled from the highchair, his favorite baby bumble bee video suddenly turned off – all of this inevitably lead to a meltdown. So - better yet, call maybe ten minutes before arriving to give your wife (or husband if the roles are switched) enough time to get your child regrouped and calmed down. When you arrive, knock on the door; call his name, whisper his name, scratch on the door while Mommy's excited voice may help pique his interest. Most children want to know what's on the other side of a door, especially if it's making noise, but this is hit or miss with autistic children. If your child can't or won't open the door himself, Mommy should help with prompts. In other words, take his hand and help him open the door – don't just do it for him.

The first night we went through the paces and expectedly Emerson was less than cooperative. I knocked and scratched at the door and finally had to open it myself at the behest of Jen who was dealing with a completely upset little boy. He didn't come to the door to open it himself, he didn't smile, and he didn't hug me. He was in complete meltdown mode on the floor. He didn't say it of course, but I could read his angry little face, "Leave me alone, I was perfectly happy in my world - eating my chicken nuggets and now I'm being forced to come and open this door for this strange person I could care less about."

I picked him up and tried to embrace him as he flipped his head back away from me. I reigned his head back in and hugged him firmly. I noticed whenever I did this he seemed to even out a bit. I would later find out one of his calming mechanisms was to have pressure put on his body. Though he would fight it at first, a firm hug would calm him down. I will go deeper into this "vestibular" therapy later in the book.

"That's all right," I said to Jen with gritting determination. "We're going to do this every night until it becomes the norm for him."

Don't be disappointed. It's not unusual for a child to melt down when exposed to a new task or behavior - especially one that requires socialization, physical contact, or affection. But these are the very elements that are missing in these children and arguably should be considered the most important.

It was not in Little Em's normal nightly pattern and we were forcing him to come out of his world, but I was determined to make it part of little Em's routine.

After a week my son began to not be so cantankerous. Sometimes I even got a smile when he peeked around the door. It took about six months to realize that keeping the lights out on my side of the mud room may help. Curiously, I found in near dark situations that he embraced me more readily. In the daylight at times he would approach while actually winching, his eyes completely shut – fighting the uncomfortable feeling in his body, but still wanting to be close. He would even cover his eyes, and then ever so slowly approach until in my arms. If a child does this it's important to let him literally walk through the discomfort into your arms, don't rush in and embrace him. You don't want to enable him to remain in one spot with his eyes closed. To make gains, keep coaxing him to come into your arms. He has to overcome the uncomfortable feeling and realize there's great reward to be had when he finally makes it to your arms.

Don't expect every night to be better than the last, and it can expectedly take months. It took me six months to figure out he was more at ease being close to my face in the dark. And six months later he would still have melt downs at the other side of the door when I came home at night, but I also had wonderful nights of hugs and eventually kisses! - A world better than being completely ignored.

You have to keep with a plan, repeat and exercise it with consistent loving repetition or *all due military precision.* I remember it being over six months since I started the greeting ritual. I came home, called, had the light out on my side and knocked excitedly on the door. All I could hear was my son's high pitch whistle of a cry on the other side. My wife put him at the door as I knocked and called his name from the other side, but despite all our effort and staging, his tantrum knocked over the dog's water bowl. Jen told me to "forget it" from the other side of the door as she lost her will for battle. Emerson had already worn her down about an hour before I showed up.

I pinched my nose and squatted down in the dark trying to figure out what to do with all my pent up frustration. Autistic children do have a number of gifts – they seem to be natural born Karate experts and when frustrated, their tantrums can bleed you out in seconds. But I dug down with my last pint of patience and soldiered on. "This is no joke," I said angrily. "Go get him and walk him to the door." I don't know what happened. Maybe my son sensed my grinding resolve from the other side of the door, or perhaps he sensed Jen's inner voice tempting her to punt him out the window, but she walked him to the door - and he opened it! He came in and didn't even hesitate in throwing his arms around me! The night and our moods were salvaged! By the way, I am kidding about the punting, but any parent who has dealt with these demonic temper tantrums is in close relations with their nefarious 'inner voices…'

My point? I can't count the number of times either Jen or I walked away from trying to work with him while the other soldiered on. And it always seemed that last try was the moment we had a break through. Don't give up, keep going. And if one or the other has had enough, it's okay to walk away. Give each other the latitude to do so without guilt.

The best part is after a year of rote, mechanical repetition Little Em actually began to open up. We began to get hugs for other things. As mentioned in chapter five, Emerson volunteered a hug when he couldn't verbally ask for the popsicle in my hand. On the flip side, Emerson soon got the bright idea to shower me with kisses and hugs when I tried to sit him down to begin a therapy session. I finally realized the little booger was attempting to get out of his therapy by showering me with affection! I'll admit it worked a couple times. All this from a child who wouldn't, no couldn't even look at me months ago.

I can say with certainty that if we had not begun the regimented stop and go and then the greeting and hugging exercises, we would not be getting these wonderful self initiated behaviors. I will also go into how we began to prompt kisses from him in the next chapter.

Emotion can be taught with structured tactics like AABA. It must be worked in with consistent repetition and it will eventually become a learned natural innate behavior.

This therapy also opens up opportunity to generalize with other family members. When "Nana or Grandpa" come over you should continue the exercise of greeting and affection. The reason I specifically bring this up is I have read some books that say to be stern with relatives and to not let them do things the child can't tolerate like unwanted hugs, kisses or other affection. I wholeheartedly don't agree. I believe the relatives must be informed and included in the Discrete Affectionate Trials and must go through the same regimen when visiting. Now both mommy and daddy can prompt their child to open the door and give a hug or kiss to Nana and Pop-pop. The relatives must be informed of what may go wrong and how to behave properly through the greeting process. Having relatives or close friends or neighbors included builds on your child's generalization skills and includes rather than excludes family.

GROUP HUG!

If he's not reacting the way you want when you come home there may still be some remedies. Everyone will be in one spot so try to take advantage of it. A-lot of the time my son would be in my wife's arms when I walked in before implementing the greeting ritual. I remember embracing him and my wife, jumping up and down while singing "group hu-ug, group hu-ug." He didn't hug back, but the song, the bouncing and the pressure of our arms brought about a smile some-times. If you get a smile – it's a start and you must keep enforcing your affection upon him with all due military precision.

I'll admit the solutions I'm illustrating won't run perfectly. Little Em didn't come running into my arms with a big hug and smile like a normally developing child, but the new tactics were giving back 100% more than what I was getting for the last few months – which was nothing. Within days and weeks I had partially elicited a wanted emotional behavior from him. Not by standing there repeating "Daddy's home!" into his ear, hoping he would one day turn around and give me a hug, but by narrowing down his stimuli and distractions, setting up an environment to create a wanted emotional behavior and prompting him to participate. We had to show him the pleasures of an embrace again and again.

I'll also admit he behaved somewhat like a robot at first. He came to the door, opened it and hugged me, sometimes with a-lot of phys-ical prompting on my part. I could tell the exercise was a mystery to him at first and he seemed to get nothing out of it. But soon the smiles and sometimes a run to the door did finally come around. He began to realize hugs did feel good, and he would smile! As I mentioned in the previous chapter, at three and a half years old – a full year and half after I started this Discrete Affectionate Trials, Emerson began requesting hugs while I worked the more advanced stop and stand in place trial. He will throw his arms around us with all this little body has to offer. Again, I can say with certainty that he would not be as affectionate as he is today if we did not work him out of his shell and make him participate in these types of Affectionate Trials.

As much work as this was, as upsetting as his little meltdowns were, we were beginning to see ever so slight improvements and this motivated us to continue. We were onto something.

Synopsis:

1. Decide what behaviors are most important to help you bond with your child. Is it a hug, a greeting at night or to just acknowledge you with a look in the eye? There are many other illustrations later in the book to help develop eye contact.

2. Trying for closeness in the dark may help your child overcome the uncomfortable feel of an embrace. If you can elicit more affection, an embrace or touch this way, work from there. Autistic children commonly like enclosed and dark spaces. Join them in their world and it may help you connect to bring them out into the light.

3. Structure and repetition, structure and repetition. You will start to see this pattern throughout the book, but repetition and structure help an autistic child function best. The trick is to integrate structure and repetition as affectionate behavior in which they must be a full participant in order to elicit the quickest results.

4. If your child is wincing, yet working towards giving a hug or other affection let him work through the discomfort. By

rushing up to hug before he makes his way to you will not allow him to overcome. Allowing him to work through will make it easier and easier for an embrace to come naturally.

5. Include family members in your Affectionate Trials. Working a two to three year old through proper affectionate social greetings will be profoundly easier than attempting this when they are older. Remember, this is the age at which they are most malleable and open to change.

CHAPTER 8

BIRTHDAYS AND HOLIDAYS, BLOWING OUT CANDLES AND UNWRAPPING GIFTS.

HOW TO PREP FOR ENJOYMENT INSTEAD OF DISAPPOINTMENT. INSTIGATING INTERACTIVE PLAY, RECEIVING KISSES AND GETTING YOUR CHILD TO ENJOY BALL PLAY.

AS I mentioned in the previous chapter, pick out things you wish your child to do that are important to you. For me it was milestones of: 1.) Becoming relevant in little Em's eyes as illustrated in the safety chapter. 2.) Greeting me at the door as mentioned in the previous chapter. 3.) Opening gifts. 4.) Blowing out birthday candles (which I found out later is typically difficult to teach autistic children) 5.) Getting kisses or hugs upon command that would later turn into genuine affection. 6.) Interactive play. 7.) Last but not least - speech.

I know everyone's list may be different, but I did try to include the most common and most rewarding things any parent would want experience with their child. Hopefully these are some of the same things you are specifically wanting to see on your wish list. Notice how the list of wants is becoming progressively intricate. As you develop your list of wants try to keep them in similar order. For instance, you are most likely not going to get speech if your child doesn't first acknowledge your presence when you come home at night. This follows Greenspan's ladder of socialization and may help you become less frustrated when it comes to wanting your child to say "Dada or Mama" too soon. Go in this general order, and pick and choose other small things you may want to correct or get from your child as you progress.

Another milestone I wanted to enjoy as a parent was watching Emerson open gifts for his birthday and Christmas. Unfortunately he was not getting the concept, nor did he care to. It was another one of those terrible moments during the holidays when we realized this. Nothing can be more disheartening than your child's lack of interest and blank stare when it comes to unwrapping presents or blowing out candles. Customs like opening gifts or blowing out candles help bring some normalcy, even hope of better things to come, but the last thing you want is your child's indifference to lie painfully naked out in front of friends and family during a birthday or holiday. Unfortunately if these normally joyous occasions aren't approached in a systematic yet creative fashion, they can become another little wedge of frustration and disconnection.

The main key to avoiding disappointment at a birthday or Christmas is to not spring any new tasks upon them when the day comes. Most kids get the idea of unwrapping gifts after the very first one. Not autistic children. The other problem is most parents are still in 'normal mode' when their child is two to three years old. Even with a diagnosis, you fail to see it coming and as a consequence they get severely disappointed.

PRACTICE FIRST!

My child is unresponsive. How can I get him to enjoy unwrapping gifts?

Wrap up his favorite toy, sing happy birthday with the lit candle and all. Expect his behavior to be off or distant. Help him unwrap it until he sees what's inside. It can even be a favorite piece of candy or licorice. Begin working these tasks months in advance. I remember Jen coming home with a new toy at least once a week, just a little something she saw while in the drug store. A pair of toddler sunglasses, or little action figurine, we're always experimenting with what would turn him on. Since he didn't do so well at his first or even second birthday, we got in the habit of wrapping the trinkets up before giving them to him.

If your child isn't ready come his real birthday then don't push it – especially in front of everyone. And don't be surprised if he acts out of sorts when everyone is around waiting for him to blow out a candle or unwrap gifts. He may have done it flawlessly for weeks, but now he's over stimulated and not cooperating. But practice makes perfect. By Emerson's third birthday we must have wrapped up his favorite toys and Pez dispensers a couple dozen times.

Blowing out the birthday candle.

I'm putting it lightly to say this can be a bit trickier than training a child to open gifts. But it's one of those tasks that results in hoots and cheers when the little one succeeds and it was important for me. We started trying to teach him how to blow out a candle eight months before his second birthday. We would light the candle, sing happy birthday and try to illustrate blowing, but the best we got was a fleeting curiosity of the flame. Overall he couldn't care less and even after eight months of trying, there was no candle blowing at his second birthday.

Perhaps we were still in some denial. Upon his second birthday the diagnosis was but a month ago, but it didn't seem like it should take so long to teach a two year old how to blow out a candle. I was obviously mistaken, but I wasn't giving up. I could have kept at him with the rote repetition of ABA, but it was getting me nowhere. One morning I got the bright idea of blowing cheerios at him. Who knows where these ideas come from, maybe it was the little boy in me, but

I was trying to illustrate the effect of blowing air. I put the cheerio between my lips and puffed. It bounced off the side of his cheek as Jen frowned with a tired tone, "What are you doing?"

"I don't know, showing how much fun it is to blow something." I did it again. This time he turned and looked at me! This was a major development. I picked up another cheerio from his tray and bounced it off his forehead with another puff. He smiled! We cheered and we clapped as he curiously acknowledged our reaction. I got another toe hold on his attention and wasn't about to let it go.

Being the mischievous little boy that I am, I kept puffing cheerios at Jen's chagrin but when he smiled she forgave all the cheerios littering the floor. Besides, Mugsey got to know when I was on a cheerio puffing binge.

It wasn't until a few months later at grandmas that I was illustrating his eye contact to my brother in law when I blew the cheerios. After puffing a couple he picked one up, put it between his lips and blew. It went straight across the table! We cheered whopped and hollered as he looked back with a smile! This is a big step for kids with his problem. Here he was: 1.) Out of his world and engaged in what another person was doing. 2.) Mimicking a behavior. 3.) Looking for reinforcement after mimicking the behavior. (We got great eye contact.) 4.) Having the proper response. (Smiling and giggling.) 5.) This was interactive behavior, not just the parallel play. 6.) Little Em was developing eye hand coordination and becoming familiar with his mouth. I know it sounds strange but exercises about the mouth help build their awareness for speech.

Emerson clumsily stuffed another cheerio between his lips as we called Jen and her mother over. They got there just in time to see another cheerio puff across the table. Everyone cheered again and I gave him a big hug. That was it for the day. Though he refused to do it anymore, we got a milestone. As I found out, autistic children will sometimes engage in flickers of lucid awareness and then retreat right back in to their world. But we got him out for just a bit.

The idea was to parlay this into blowing a candle, but things don't always go as planned. As the weeks passed he began to blow the chee-rios more often. We would over react and clap and in return we would get a smile out of him. I kept bringing the candle out and trying the transition from blowing cheerios to blowing a flame. He would look curiously at the flame and we actually got him to blow on maybe two occasions, but the mistake I made was letting his little fingers near the flame. I thought it would be good for him to learn "HOT", to realize under this controlled environment what the word meant would help him when there was a greater threat of burning himself say by a stove or hot food. His fingers only went close to the flame as I exclaimed "Hot, hot!" He got the hint and never had his fingers too close, but what it did was make him fearful of the flame all together. Now every time I took the candle out to practice he cowered away. Shish.

There was another side effect of the cheerio training. He soon realized he could just spit without a cheerio! Shish again. Well, the bad side is obvious, however, now we had a child who would spit and then laugh like it was funniest thing he had ever experienced once he realized he had our attention. Out of the two and half years of his life I had yet to see him actually laugh! This was huge for me and Jen. He would look to us with his lips pursed; he'd spit and then laugh and giggle looking for our reaction at the same time. I know it was a bad habit, but I was getting eye contact, play indicators, true interaction that I never got before. It was wonderful to have him in the room, not just physically but mentally as well! He was obviously trying to get me to play with him. And now that he was paying attention to me, I could work on curbing the spitting behavior. I was stern with the word stop and I could tell he understood as my stop and go therapy was of assistance here. I also began to use the word "Gentle," and blow softly on his face after he spit so he could feel the experience of the softer blowing air I was striving for on the lit candle.

One of the therapists approached us at the end of his school day to say he was spitting. She remarked at how unsanitary it was and how it needed to be immediately corrected, but she also shook her head and said it was all she could do to discipline him because she realized he was attempting to instigate play without the ability of verbal communication. She too was pleasantly shocked at his eye contact and impish giggles after spitting. He was vying for her attention. We agreed it was a great progression, though my interactive therapy had developed an unexpected curve. When I explained what I had tried to do and the direction it went she suggested I try blowing on a cotton ball in front of him to illustrate wind. "It may have circumvented the spitting," she said. Great idea I thought, but too late for that. (Off the record, I still think spitting cheerios at each other was much more fun than blowing on cotton balls.)

We had to focus on curbing the spitting for some time and the lit candle still upset him when we placed it in front of him. I was very disappointed, but there was still another six months until his third birthday. We managed to control the spitting by either ignoring the behavior (not rewarding him by paying attention) or softly saying "Stop, not funny." I also kept trying to illustrate how to blow without spitting.

About three months went by before I decided to bring the candle back out. I figured we were starting at scratch, but just as I lit the wick he blew it out! Jen and I went into cheers like the final touchdown from the 2008 Giants vs. Patriots Super bowl. We lit the candle again and he succinctly blew it out again! We did it three more times, then every morning for the next couple weeks.

It's a puzzlement how things can be so arduous and difficult, seem like we're getting nowhere then out of the blue it clicks. It took over a year to imprint this behavior. After starting well before the age of two, he was finally ready to blow out a candle for his third birthday. This is another example of how creativity, persistence and patience will eventually eat through what seems to be impenetrable barriers. We pushed forward, got set back, had to correct an unexpected behavior (spitting); take time off from the candle, but in the end it finally happened. In my mind, all I wanted was for him to blow a candle out on his birthday. But through our persistence we got so much more: Emerson developed better eye contact, a flirting grin (just before spitting) and a giggle that fluttered my stomach. As much heartbreak as I was weathering, my son was ever so slowly starting to emerge from the blond haired distant eyed little stranger in my house.

Getting Kisses:

Getting kisses from an autistic child requires a few things in order to work them into it. How do you get a child who is uncomfortable with close contact to tolerate let alone reciprocate kisses? Like getting hugs when coming home at night, a kiss from your child is another behavior that can really 'turn the worm' and help keep you in the game trying for your little one.

I'll remind you that Emerson regarded me as completely irrelevant. I was nothing more than a fixture in the way, a piece of living furniture that he had to navigate around. He didn't answer to his name, turned away when I got in his face and his eyes even rolled white in his head when I held his cheeks to look at me. My experience is at best lots of parents simply rain kisses down on the child in hopes that someday they will reciprocate. At worst, they "protect" or insulate their child from touching in order to keep them calm and regulated. As I mentioned earlier, insulating your child from certain affectionate social interaction will simply make your job of integrating him infinitely harder down the road.

As I'll admit when kisses were first instilled into Emerson it was little more than a habit we implanted in him. It meant nothing to him and he did it as a means of getting something else he wanted. But as I professed earlier in the book, he soon came to realize that he liked it. Not only does the exercise of drawing out kisses from your child help you cope. It is probably the most important therapy your child can receive. Remember, don't expect a therapist to work kisses in as the discrete trial itself.

Again I used the wonderful cheerio as a therapeutic tool. You can use any other sort of candy, cracker or licorice that they simply must have. I started out by handing him one cheerio at a time while attempting to get him to 'mand' (request more) by tapping the tips of his fingers together. Signing is a typical way to bridge autistic children into speech so at the time we were trying this.

He would tap the tips of his fingers together and I would hand him a single cheerio. To get him to look at me I put the cheerio between my lips. He seemed to have no problem grabbing the cheerio from my lips…. Hmmm. When he reached for the next one I held his hands and moved in close. He turned away. We went back and forth a while until he finally got brave enough to take the cheerio from my lips with his. Our whoops and hollers made him smile just a bit as I could tell he was somewhat mystified what the big deal was. Interestingly, I could see his eyes look painfully to the side to avoid eye contact as he approached to take the cheerio with his mouth. But that was okay, he was working through the discomfort for a reward.

Soon I had Jen doing the same thing and it was becoming a game to him. We kept smooching him when he took the cheerio from our lips with his and repeating "kiss!"

Soon we were getting kisses upon request. Yes, they were limp fishy lips from him, but this was still great progression as he was becoming more and more comfortable with the close contact. I also noticed his eyes were less averted or rolled away as he approached us. We soon began to overemphasize the "MMM" letting our lips sort of vibrate on his to illustrate the sound. Many autistic children have muscle control problems when it comes to the mouth and lips, as does Emerson. By getting Emerson to hum back at our kisses we were inadvertently helping build lip control and mouth to sound awareness. I would hum in an animated higher pitch to get his attention during a kiss. His turned away eyes began to look at me while we were nose to nose and eventually his eyes would light up with mine.

It took months, but kisses soon became part of Emerson's natural everyday behavior. Developing exercises and trials for this kind of closeness is not something you can expect from a therapist. This type of therapy is best derived from the parents.

At nearly three and a half he will kiss us upon request and even make a game of it. He will smack his lips against our cheeks in a comical overzealous way. Even though he has no speech, it's become obvious he now loves kisses. If your child has similar aversion towards close contact and you don't push similar specific affectionate exercises through rote ritualistic repetition you won't experience this wonderful progression.

INSTIGATING INTERACTIVE PLAY:

As mentioned in the Therapy Chapter, some people refer to this as Floor Time or Greenspan's approach to therapy. It's where you get down at your child's level and attempt to play with them to build the relationship. But where to begin? Most times I would find myself at a loss. He would hold the toy trains too close to his eyes and stare at the wheels, line them up in row, etc etc. I soon found myself simply correcting behavior and not actually interacting like I should. I wasn't being a very fun playmate. This is one of the reasons Floor Time therapy is so hard. As a parent you keep noticing how your child isn't playing properly and it simply gets more and more upsetting. But sometimes you can take things that you would normally want to steer away from and use them to your advantage. For instance:

CEILING FANS, FROM BANE TO THERAPY.

As with many autistic children, spinning wheels and fans are the hypnotic vehicle that drives them further into their abyss. At first Jen and I did everything we could to keep Emerson from staring incessantly at the whirling ceiling fan blades. Then one day over my sister's house, her husband Bob picked Emerson up after noticing how he stared at the ceiling fan in the kitchen. Bob took my son's hand and helped him pull on the chain to change its speed. When it clicked, Bob let out a clown like wide eyed guffaw and Emerson unexpectedly erupted in laughter. Not only that, he looked Bob in the eyes for more. My brother in law obliged and the domino's of clicks and laughs ensued.

"All children love fans," he said as if it were dismissive common knowledge. "We used to do this with Emily." This man has a natural easy way with children. I don't know if it's the long graying hair or his trusting quiet demeanor, but it worked. I asked to try it and Emerson had the same laugh with me as he did with Bob. Well not quite as much, but enough. *Whew.*

This type of interaction accomplishes a number of things. 1.) It requires your participation. 2.) The child and parent have to touch and hold each other as part of the exercise. 3.) Whooping and laughing in reaction to the chain being pulled helps break down the touch barriers and neatly impels close facial interaction. 4.) Clicking the chain and changing speeds or turning on and off the light give the child cause and reaction understanding. 5.) It may help later toward speech as it did for Emerson. He would stand in the middle of the room and point to the fan. I would point along with him and enunciate F-A-N. He would try to make the sound before I picked him up to pull on the chain.

TRAIN SET

When I did try to connect with Emerson while playing with his toys I was systematically ignored. What I did find is many children – even autistic children can have the knack for wanting what they don't have. So I would try to find another favorite toy of his and begin to play with it on my own, but very much in his view. This worked sometimes, but it would usually turn out with him simply trying to take it for his own instead of playing with me. It did open opportunities to teach sharing, but it was still less interactive play and not much fun for anyone.

Emerson as well as many other autistic children loves Thomas The Train. Don't ask me exactly what it is, (because he can't tell me), but there's something about the wide eyed plastic faced trains that fascinated him. So we got him a rather cheap plastic battery operated train set and set it up in the play room. Very small, it was only about three feet long and two feet wide oval track, but it did have a remote control that made train noises when it stopped and started. You could put little logs in the back cars and even fit a matchbox car.

This worked great. He soon learned the cause and effect of the remote and the little train provided lots of opportunity to play together since it would easily be knocked off the tracks. In my opinion, a little toy like this really helped him learn to play with the train correctly and allowed me to sit on the other side of the track and participate with him. I could load the cars as they went by, help put a car back on the rail, etc. Soon he began to set up little houses around the track and such. No speech or eye contact, but we were playing together. It was no longer just me trying to correct improper behavior.

INTERACTIVE BALL PLAY: PROGRESSING FROM UNWANTED BOLTING TO INTERACTIVE HIDE AND SEEK AND EVENTUALLY TO PLAYING BALL:

Another milestone dads dream of is tossing a ball back and forth with their son. I am no exception and I remember the first time I showed Emerson a ball and attempted to play with him. I gently tossed the ball just inches from him. It hit him in the chest and dropped to the floor. He didn't instinctively pick it up or realize I was attempting to connect with him. He just stood with the heart wrenching blank face. I tried to get him to play for months and months. I rolled, threw and spun softballs, whiffle-balls and kick-balls, but nothing interested him. What a heartbreaker. *So how do I get my son interested in proper ball play?* For Emerson it took a combination of hardcore prompting and some creative linking towards interactive play.

Let's do the fun part first. It's a bit round about, but it may help you cleverly introduce ball play. As you already know, Emerson loves to bolt and it's common with many autistic children. One of the things that can be done to make his natural inclination to run is play hide and seek. You're probably thinking it's a way too advanced concept for

your child. It was for Emerson as well, but here is where it's important
for both parents to be involved. Holding Emerson's hand, Jen would
run Emerson to a dark corner of the house or in a closet all while
verbally expressing her excitement along with the general sounds of
hiding (whispering and crouching down.) I would of course be the
one opening the door with a roar, Jen would scream and they would
run hand in hand to the next hiding spot. You may wish to temper the
loud noises if your child is averted to startling sounds, but for us the
sounds helped keep him focused on what was going on around him.
It took weeks, no months for Emerson to really seem to get it, but he
soon became familiar with all the hiding spots and began to follow Jen
as they ran to hide without having to be led by the hand. Furthermore,
as time went on he would smile and chortle as I pounced in on the
hiding spot and began to chase them. I still had no luck in getting
any interest from him in playing with a ball until I got the bright idea
of having Jen give him a ball as he was in mid run. This didn't take
immediately as he would simply throw the ball away to run, but one
day he finally held onto a miniature little football and began to run
with it in his hands like an over confident running back. I started
trying to take the ball as he ran which only made him giggle and try
to run away more.

It was great! I had my first glimmer of interactive play with a ball
about three or four months after the age of three. He looked like a
natural running with the football and he got so much joy out of shrug-
ging off my mocking little tackles. For the first time since his diagnosis
I had hope that he could possibly go into some sports. At nearly the
age of four, running from me with a ball in his hands while giggling
and laughing is now one of his favorite play activities. I know this is a
very roundabout way to get him interested in ball play and it did take
quite a while, but it worked.

As far as getting him to interactively catch and throw a ball was and
still is a much more generic type of therapy. Emerson's attention span
and drive to bolt made it impossible at first to attempt simple one on
one ball play. I needed to kneel behind him while Jen would bounce a

light kick ball sized ball to his chest. I had to physically prompt him by saying "hands out" and hold him by the wrists or hands to keep them open. He seemed to only want to punch the ball away.

I'll admit this was not much fun and many sessions didn't last more than a minute or two, but we worked on it nearly every night. By the age of three and a half he began to independently pick the ball up and throw it to me!

These are the things dad needs to be there for. Like I said in the beginning of the book, autism is malleable. At first it's like trying to bend cold steel, but with as much technique as tenacity you can accomplish amazing things. Be creative. If some of the techniques I have illustrated don't work, fine tune them to match your household, try round about strategies. As you can tell by my story of getting Emerson interested in ball play and blowing out candles – the road to our destination was not a straight or continuous line.

Synopsis

Let's review. So far you have received tools to:

1.) Become relevant to your child while developing safety exercises and listening ability.
2.) Shown a regimen to elicit hugs and greetings when coming home.
3.) Develop and practice important milestones such as opening gifts, blowing out candles, getting hugs and kisses and last but not least, interactive ball play.

Hopefully after implementing some of these strategies your child is looking less like an unreachable stranger. Don't give up; progression doesn't happen overnight, especially with autistic children. This book is a quick read, but these strategies should be worked on for months and need to be implemented in daily consistent fashion. I've read books where they talk of their child figuring out a discrete trial that took little Em over a year to master. No matter how slow, progression is the key. So long as these exercises start to crack autisms shell, you're on the right path. Just keep hammering.

Let's keep going. There are still many important things to cover that will enable you to connect with your child and restore some hope in your household.

CHAPTER 9

SPEAKING

ONE of the most disappointing things about autism is some children's limited or complete inability to develop speech. There's no set time frame for autistic children to develop speech. Some children learn at the normal timeframe as those diagnosed with asperger's syndrome. Others never say a word their entire lives and then there's everything in between. The therapies can range in style and intensity from simplistic speech lessons to physical prompting of the mouth and jaw.

There are whole books and professions focused solely on the development of speech. There are many theories and therapies to assist and coax speech. Tactics like sign language, PECS *Picture Exchange Communication System*, 'computer talk and go' and so on. For me to hope to accomplish something new and dramatic or think I could teach all there is to know about eliciting speech within a chapter would be absurd. What this book is about is helping you the parent to bond and understand your child. To develop empathy so you become less frustrated and more compassionate with their condition. I admit this is a short chapter, but it's not a cop out. On the contrary, as you have read in the previous chapters, all the exercises you are implementing are building blocks for speech. Being able to hold your child's attention, having your voice and face become significant to them, developing emotion and interactive play, all those things are bringing your worlds together and opening up avenues for your child to desire communication. My hope is the drills and training at home to build family bonds provide a foundation to help your child focus when it comes time to work with a therapist on speech.

On that note, I don't know any parent who doesn't repeat "Mama" or "Dada" more than any other word in the hopes it will be their child's first words. As much as receiving a heartfelt greeting at the door is a cornerstone of bonding with your children, so are the words 'Mama' or 'Dada' from your child. Unfortunately, however, those words are typically some of the later words learned by autistic children who do develop speech. Once I learned this, it helped me not to become so frustrated whenever I tried to get little Emerson to say it.

Autistic children are naturally indifferent to people and more attracted to things. As a result you should have much more success in getting him to speak for toys, food or actions he wants to do. I figured this out by accident as I go back to the ceiling fan. One of his favorite things to look at and play with, he would pull me out of my chair and point to the fan. He wanted me to raise him up and pull the chain again. This time I sat and pointed with him and said "FFFFAAAANNNN." I over enunciated the F and I saw him intently watching my mouth! He couldn't understand how to put his lower lip under his front teeth to pronounce 'F', but he started to "SSshhhhaa". He pointed at the fan still, wanting me to bring him up, but I kept pointing as well, letting him know I understood what he wanted, but I kept over enunciating 'Fan!"

For the first time he was trying to say the word. After a few 'SSsshhaa's' I cheered and let him pull the string. The trick is to find something your child likes or wants so badly that they're willing to work for it.

I had been missing the point for a long time. I was repeating Mama and Dada for months and months, but here I find something he wants – I make him work for five minutes and suddenly he's actually trying to say the word; an unbelievable leap in the right direction with a slight change in my behavior. The funny thing is I think I felt the same joy watching him try to say the word 'fan' as I would have if he said 'Dada.' Well, maybe not, but it seemed close.

Having Emerson work at saying "fan" while having fun clicking it on and off was one of the more therapeutic things for both of us. This was different than the "go or stop!" he would repeat while working with me outside. The dynamic of having him in my arms in close quarters was a new bridge I was building. Plus, with him focused on the fan helped distract him from the uncomfortable feeling that close contact brought about.

To our dismay Emerson was diagnosed with apraxia just before three and a half years of age. It's a neurological condition that affects their ability to produce the precise movements of the mouth, lips and tongue to produce speech. The condition is not fully understood and can be easily mistaken for simple speech delay. The difference between speech delay and apraxia is if there is a wide gap between understanding verbal requests (receptive understanding), and their ability to produce their own speech. Normal children typically learn to produce speech within a certain small gap of receptive verbal understanding. Furthermore, when a normal child learns speech, they can quickly learn to correct their mouth, lip and tongue movements to produce the proper enunciation. Children stricken with apraxia have a much more difficult time self correcting the fine nuances of the mouth to make the proper sounds. For instance Emerson continually says "Dye Dye," instead of "Bye Bye." I keep getting in his face and make the "ba" lip movement. At times he will repeat "ba" but can't associate it to saying "bye bye." This also explains why after months of work he still has problems with the "F" in "fan".

This diagnosis was of course another punch in the gut, but it made sense. I could see little Em trying to mouth the words only to see them get lost somewhere behind his eyes. To this day when I see him try to say the words it brings me to tears. But understanding this condition has changed my demeanor from short fused frustration to empathy and compassion. It's increased my ability to focus, get in front of him and work with the movements of his mouth tongue and lips. I guess what I'm getting at here, as a constant theme in this book is under-standing the nuances of your child's condition lessens frustration and helps you focus in a constructive empathetic manner.

Interestingly enough, even though Emerson was diagnosed with apraxia, his first words were "go!, out and run!" which were the things we were focusing on at home, proving the tactics Jen and I employed were having positive side effects of speech development. Many thera-pists will say it's best to first work on nouns instead of verbs, but I disagree. Associating a word with an action, especially an action they want (like turning the bane of unwanted bolting to a cooperative playful "run or go!") can have a great positive effect on their learning ability. As I discussed earlier in the book, Emerson's first words were of action, things he wanted to do. In my experience, it's exercises that completely involve the child's participation that proved the most successful.

We are still in the process of inciting speech from him and we work at it every opportunity we get. Though currently he is in the stage of echolalia we have high hopes for great improvement.

CHAPTER 10

ENABLING, TEMPER TANTRUMS AND BITING. UNDERSTANDING AND CONTROLLING OVER STIMULATION AND DESTRUCTIVE BEHAVIOR.

THE title is a mouthful and a-lot to cover, but much of understanding and dealing with temper tantrums, over stimulation and destructive behavior all falls under the same umbrella. It's all dysfunctional behavior.

Parental Enabling and Temper Tantrums: Here's a prime example of enabling for no reason. When our son was diagnosed at 23 months he was only a few weeks away from moving from the Yellow Birds classroom to the Purple Cats in his day care. He was about to "graduate" from a class of one to two year olds into a class room of two to three year olds. We immediately informed our daycare of our son's diagnosis. "He has PDD NOS." My wife said.

"Oh." The Director's eyes lit up then looked away. "Do you want me to hold him back with the one year olds?" Whenever we told anyone of his diagnosis it seemed they either physically or metaphorically took a step back, their hands went up and a barrier formed around us and our son. Their widened assessing eyes said, *Give him room, he has a problem.*

I even saw it in my wife. When Emerson started acting out or having a temper tantrum, she would kind of sit back and relegate it to his diagnosis. "Well, he's autistic. I hear it's common for them to have temper tantrums." It's called enabling, and my parental instincts told me we had to do just the opposite.

At the time we already began to experience success with the focused proper affectionate greeting exercise, but had yet to instill the stop and go strategies. I felt letting him stay in his day dreams and other worlds and not pushing forward would just be not only throwing away the key, but letting the lock rust.

We poured through the web sites and found our instincts were right. It's too easy as a parent to give your child what he wants before they really ask for it, or give into inappropriate behavior. But that was all about to change.

When breakfast came the cheerios and banana puree was always there in front of him. Life was easy. He didn't need to communicate. I scooped up the cheerios and puree and put them on table out of reach. "We need to get out of the habit of giving him everything," I said.

He stared at it for a while then the big lower lip started to show. "Here we go," I said. He started flapping and crying. "Cheerios?" We said pointing. "You want cheerios?" We kept pointing as he kept getting more upset.

I could see Jen, her eyes weary from all we were enduring. "Can't we just give it to him?"

Emerson ratcheted up his fit and began to cry uncontrollably, it seemed there would be no way of getting our point across. The battle of wills was hitting critical mass. "No," I said as I grabbed my cup of coffee. "Ignore him."

Maybe we were asking too much I thought. But most children at twenty four months of age can actually ask for cheerios. My son had no speech whatsoever and all I wanted was for him to point.

I tried to watch the news and eat breakfast as my son wailed. I repeatedly turned and pointed to the pile of cheerios on the table. By now he looked at me in disbelief that I had lost my swami cap and could no longer read his mind. I kept pointing and finally it came.

His hand reached out toward the cheerios. "Very good!" I pointed, "Cheerios?"

He then made a low begging moan and his index finger began to point – sort of. "Yes!" It was good enough for me and Jen grabbed the bowl and put it in front of him.

"Shish! Don't give him the whole bowl!" See, it's a hard habit to break. "We got him to do it once. We have to keep repeating it so it sinks in."

As unnerving and painful as it is to hear your child's crying, as utterly enraging it is to battle his will and his temper tantrums it is an unfortunate necessity in order to open proper communication. The sooner a child is taught that behavior other than tantrums get them what they want, the sooner a semblance of sanity will prevail.

Temper tantrums are nothing new for any child, however, parents of autistic children are hamstrung. Autistic children may have over-sensitive smell or hearing, become completely upset when they see something out of order. Things we could never imagine may be intolerable for them. Sometimes we have to be super sleuths when it comes to these meltdowns. We may think they hate the chicken nuggets put in front of them because of a sudden meltdown, but in reality the smell of the peanut butter and jelly sandwich your making yourself that to them smells rancid.

Their frustration levels can be extreme as they realize they can't communicate their wishes or what it is that's upsetting them. This is what makes dealing with the darker side of autism so difficult. With normal developing children you can pretty much figure out what's bothering them via normal communication. Furthermore, they're not dealing with the quirky sensory issues that are so alien to us. More and more research is showing that the autistic meltdowns are a "learned behavior". I have mixed emotions on this perspective. I've heard of children flipping out for "no reason at all" then come to realize they are holding their head like it's about to explode and flipping out because the hum and flicker of the room's fluorescent lighting is driving them insane. How would you behave if you were in a strange place, unable to communicate as some incessant buzzing and strobe light is over-whelming your senses? You would probably react much the same way. The point I'm trying to make here is to have compassion and do your best to work constructively through it.

Floor flopping and head flipping back: I know this was addressed and discussed to some degree later in the Stop For Safety's Sake Chapter, but I think it needs to be discussed in further detail. Body flopping and head flipping are typical tactics of any child who doesn't want to do something or go where you want them to. Emerson was no exception. When he didn't want to do something he would flop in the ground and go limp. This can be a particularly distressing behavior from autistic children because their thousand mile stare off to the distance or through the floor can really be disturbing to see. Their limp limbs pour through your grip and their head reels back. Head flipping was no different. I remember coming home and taking him up in my arms. Little Em was so averted to me that his head would reel back with such force that he nearly flipped out of my arms a number of times.

This is their way of saying "get off, I can't stand to be touched." I guess there's three ways to go here. 1.) You cannot address it at all and hope it goes away (which is enabling it to continue). 2.) You can let them down and attempt Greenspan's approach by trying to figure out a way to get into their world without upsetting them. Develop a closer relationship and hope the head flipping and body flopping disappear or, 3.) You can do what I did and not tolerate it. When in my arms I would real him back up and correct him with a firm "Stop it!" I know I will most likely catch lots of flak for that because the argu-ment is I'm now making close contact seem like a punishment or even more unpleasant. I argue that I'm simply enforcing proper behavior and correcting intolerable conduct. The head flipping was nullified as Emerson soon realized being picked up and hugged was something he would simply have to tolerate. And as you read in the previous chapter about setting up hugs and kisses, the affectionate acts soon became part of his daily regimen and integrated into his being. I don't believe in enabling a child to stay cocooned, not allowing extended family members to touch or hug your child because they have an aversion to close contact. You must show and put them through the family habits of affection as discussed in the previous chapter as soon as possible or their aversion to touch and affection will simply grow deeper roots.

I also applied zero tolerance as I mentioned earlier when it came to his tactic of body flopping to the floor when he didn't want to do something. For Emerson, it was not only a physical but also a mental trip back into his nether world, the connection to the here and now would be switched off, his face would go emotionless, his body would flop and his glare would remain towards the floor. I find it uncanny how he can seemingly switch his cognition on and off like that. I remember when he did this to Jen's mom. She tried to work with him, to pick him up as he kept resisting and flopping. "Get up, now," I barked from a distance. I previously had this under control, but I later realized he seems to try this on anyone he can. Once he realized this was not a negotiation or a wrestling match he jumped up, the lucidity returned to his eyes and his cognition returned.

My suggestion is when your child first attempts this it should be dealt with in a swift overwhelming fashion. Flopping is one of those things that can escalate. They go limp and pull away from your grip. They flop half way to the ground, you try to pick them up, they flop more, you now use both hands, they start to pull for the floor and resist further with crying or screaming. My advice is the second that child begins to flop, you bend down with an extremely firm "stop!" accompanied by a firm picking up of his body. This immediately nullifies the escalation process. They will be righted back up on their feet in abrupt speed. It may be enough to shock him out of any consideration for ramping up further resistance and diving into this nether world. If he decides to melt down with a crying fit, I used the tactic of immediately putting him in a place that had no toys or other stimulation and told with hand motions and verbal discipline how flopping would not be tolerated. I would then put my palm out so he knew he had to stay in the corner until he calmed down. It took a bit of doing, but he soon realized time out was no fun. I believe much of disciplining an autistic child is much the same as a normal child in many instances. Give them credit for understanding that they are not behaving correctly. The complications are from their increased frustration level at an inability to communicate, our confusion at attempting to figure out what's wrong and our fright of disciplining a child with special needs.

Biting: Not an uncommon trait of normally developing children, but once again it seems to be ramped up with autistic children. And once again parents and caregivers seem hamstrung when it comes to correcting an overly nasty biting habit.

What is the number one deterrent to any unacceptable behavior out there? CONSEQUENCES. If you could go into a bank today and rob it of $50,000 with no consequences, absolutely none, you would at least consider it and a large percentage of us would do it! And we are normally functioning adults. Imagine an autistic child who finds the real world of little interest and who experiences little or no consequences when biting. As a matter of fact they're probably rewarded in some way because the other child that was bothering them runs away or the parent who just got bit lets them go (which is what they wanted). So how do you begin to correct this? I say bite them back. I know this sounds preposterous, but hear me out because we are not only going to show immediate and swift consequence we are also going to teach and build empathy. Let's look at the definition of empathy: In paraphrasing, it's the action of being aware of, understanding and most importantly vicariously feeling the experience of another person. I believe empathy is something that must be taught - especially in autistic children. Empathy is one of the finest learned social skills, it builds social connection as well as internal checks and balances against unacceptable behavior. It's one of the key human qualities that separates us from the rest of the animals. As they say, nature is not cruel it's just indifferent. You have to build their heart from the ground up. So, let's go through a scenario. Your child bites you. You purposefully say "Oowww!" Very loud and in their face. If your child has the skills to understand reparation like "I'm sorry" and to kiss the bite mark then enforce it along with a possible time out. If they don't and they're simply biting and still attempting to bolt from you as you try to complete the above corrections then more swift measures must take place to get their attention and enforce corrections.

If you're bit from a child who has not learned to or is not receptive to "normal correction" then immediately nip them back just enough to get the shocked look on their face. As they are crying you immediately go into compassion mode, you point to the spot they got bit and say "booboo" and give it a kiss. Then say "I'm sorry" and have them go through the same motions on you. Have them point to the bite mark that they made and repeat 'booboo' if they're able and attempt to have them kiss it better.

I know the critics are going to point at the mixed signals of consequences and compassion, but you're illustrating: 1.) The behavior will not be tolerated. 2.) That their bite really does hurt and they don't want to be bit back. 3.)What a booboo is and that mommy or daddy will make it better. 4.) He has to provide reparation for his wrong doing - i.e. kiss the booboo better and say, "I'm sorry" if he is able.

It's a process of immediate consequence, developing self awareness of how he hurts others, then reparation for his wrong doing. Simply telling a child "no biting" isn't about to curb him, let alone develop any semblance of empathy or compassion.

Over Stimulation and Destructive Behavior: Before our IEP meeting we met with an Occupational Therapist to obtain our own assessment of his condition. As she approached Emerson he squeezed his eyes shut so tight that his teeth showed. He resisted and cried in her arms and our hearts sank into our stomachs. Behavior like this shuts a man down, makes him turn to his primal urges to stop this outrageous behavior. I will admit I would simply walk away and leave it to my wife to calm him down at first. I was afraid of myself, of doing something I would regret. I know this sounds terrible and it is, but for anyone who has experienced the maniacal tantrum of an autistic child knows just how embarrassing, unnerving and infuriating this behavior can be, especially when you have no understanding of why they are behaving so terribly. There's no reasoning with the child, you hold them and they fight and scream even louder. They don't look you in the eyes for feed back; they don't hear your whispers of parental assurance. No, they head-but you under the chin. Your tongue is numb and bleeding and as you hold your mouth he shins you in the balls. His aimless thrashing seems to hit with the uncanny accuracy of a ninja. And people wonder why parents of autistic children don't go out to public places very much.

They were hard lessons, but I became an expert in juvenile ju-jitsu. Jen was no match for him, but I soon mastered the moves to envelope him in a manner that wouldn't harm either of us. We knew it was called pressure therapy, but that didn't stop the embarrassing glares to his screams as it seemed I was crushing him.

The therapist before us kept working with him, fearlessly gathering him up as he writhed away from her. Meanwhile she began to explain exactly what was going on. She peeled his behavior apart and helped us get inside his mind. She explained his anxiety level, how he couldn't learn about his environment until he could 'self regulate' or calm himself down. How putting him in situations like this was a necessary evil so he could develop the social cues and learn how to control himself. (This goes back to Greenspan's theory that a child needs to be capable of self regulating their emotions before going to the next level of emotion and socialization.)

She gave an example. "Can you remember a time in your childhood that you were so upset over a subject in school? You can't stand the class, you hate the teacher, you're frustrated and upset about the bad grade you got. Was it easy to learn? Absolutely not. Your anxiety level was way too high and distracting."

"Well," she explained further. "It's infinitely more intense than that. When an autistic child is exposed to new surroundings, a new face, a place with lots of disorder, their anxiety level sky rockets. They have none of the tools to read people's faces or other social cues to help them self regulate and behave properly." The fact this woman could still multitask despite Emerson's disturbing behavior made me keener than ever to her analysis. She had obviously seen this hundreds of times and this is what happens when my son goes to unfamiliar surroundings. This is where autism really rears its ugly head, but now I began to understand why sensory rooms were so important and my empathy level and patience for Emerson's behavior increased tenfold. These are the things I needed to understand as a father if I were to connect with him, his condition and stay the course. My outlook towards Em's behavior was slowly turning from utter short fused frustration to compassion. This was about the time I began to really understand and become ever more defensive of my son and his condition as well.

I remember the therapist saying, "This is why it's so important to get him help early."

"Because he will just stay the same and not grow out of it." I said finishing her sentence.

"No," she continued. "He will actually get worse, because the older he gets, the more that's expected of him. He will become more set in his ways and he will have recessed further into his world. It's what is comfortable for him and it will become increasingly harder to teach and bring him out of it. Worse yet, the older he gets, the stronger he gets as well." She said while struggling with him. "If you think trying to control a two and a half year old is tough, imagine a five or seven year old."

I never imagined being intimidated by a five year old, but that was before getting a one-two in the groin and under the chin from my two year old son.

As we spoke to the therapist at the end of my son's assessment we left him to wander about the room to explore. Out of the corner of my eye I noticed him approaching with his eyes winced closed and his arms outstretched. I brought the therapists attention to observe his behavior. He finally stopped, opened his eyes and pursed his lips with a shy grin. I knew what was coming.

He spit then laughed. "No spitting," I said with firm discipline. But he ran away while gleefully looking back!" I embarrassingly explained to the therapist the candle blowing therapy via cheerios and how it had run a bit off course.

She smiled, "You're being creative and that's great. Though it's not sanitary and we do have to curb it, he is trying to communicate with you, which is awesome! This is obviously his way of saying he wants you to play with him. You don't want to shut him down because a-lot of autistic children don't have the skill set to communicate or even desire play with other people. The fact he's come up with some means – and want for communication is a milestone."

I never thought I'd be so proud of my son's spitting.

CONTROLLING OVER STIMULATION AT PARTIES AND OTHER SOCIAL SETTINGS:

The 'stop and go' safety exercise discussed in the safety chapter can work wonders when it comes to bringing an autistic child down a few notches when they become suddenly over stimulated. Removing a child from an overwhelming situation and giving them tasks to stop cantankerous behavior is known as **Redirecting** and can have dramatic positive effects that can salvage the situation. It can help you stay at the parties longer and possibly even allow you to stay at the restaurant without having to leave early with a screaming child and your tail between your legs.

Somehow this tactic simply dawned on me out of necessity. We went to a party where Emerson immediately went deaf to any verbal commands. He began stomping like Godzilla through some toys all the other children were playing with. Instead of repeating myself over and over and getting frustrated with a child flopping from my grip - (in front of everyone), I took him by the hand and simply began walking him through his stop and go paces. He would cry when he realized the jig was up, but it's not simply putting him a corner to cry and act out further. He had a task at hand – he had to follow my commands of stop and go. And when we stopped, I made him look me in the eye before moving again. I also repeated the word "gentle" when I pointed back in the direction of the other children. The exercise originally meant save his life had the added benefit. It became a tool to rein him back in from the terrible monster of over stimulation.

That day I must have put him through the first floor circuit of my neighbor's house at least a dozen times. Yes, he pitched some fits for being pulled away. However, by the end of the day the minute he saw my hand out for "the walk", he would capitulate and calm down. How interesting.

LIVING IN A BOX – VESTIBULAR AND PROPRIOCEPTIVE INPUT/THERAPY.

I put these two terms together because they tend to go hand in hand. Ever heard the term, "buy your child an expensive toy and they play with the box?" For some autistic children this couldn't be more true.

The vestibular system tells the body where it is compared to their surroundings. It has to do with balance and movement. I know Emerson would turn deaf and lose any ability to self regulate especially when he got outdoors to a baseball field – he would simply run and keep running. Key indicators of a child who needs vestibular therapy is:

- Decreased eye contact.
- Decreased attention span.
- Repetitive movement.

Therapeutic Activities that help: playground swings, rocking chair, bouncer or trampoline.

I will say the use of a bouncer has been of great help to Emerson. When we first tried it out it made us realize how bad his condition was, but we managed to take what began as a nightmare and turned it into a great therapeutic tool that we all enjoy. We got it as a gift from my brother in law (he would do anything for his nephew). It was over the top, nearly the size of those rental units. It could fit about six screaming over excited little toddlers and even had a slide. We brought it to the neighborhood Halloween party – about 4 months after Emerson's diagnosis. We were still devastated and more aware than ever about his problematic behavior, but had yet to begin instituting the stop and go therapy. Emerson had fleeting interest in the bouncer when we set it up at home and we had high hopes the other kids would help keep his attention. Sure enough we set it up and all the kids pounced all over it, but Emerson just kept running away towards the fields. The other children overwhelmed him and he exhibited quite an aversion to crowds. We couldn't get him in the bouncer unless we physically put him in, then he simply crawled out and bolted for the hills. Emerson didn't want anything to do with the other kids, the bouncer or us. He just wanted to run away and not look back. I had to keep retrieving Emerson as Jen watched all the other neighborhood kids enjoy the new bouncer the way it was supposed to be enjoyed. She broke down in tears as I retrieved Little Em who was grunting and whining. We had to leave the party early.

It was one of the countless lower points we experienced after his diagnosis, however, we set the bouncer up at home and introduced it daily with just the two of us as his company. We managed to just fit it in our garage. With the doors closed, we gained control of the environment and were able to keep him rather contained from bolting. Soon he began to smile and run about in the bouncer with us.

Now, a year later, he loves the bouncer, but we had to work at it. We had to physically keep placing him into the bouncer after he would simply run away. On a daily basis we would blow it up and spend time tumbling, throwing balls, falling down and laughing – we did whatever it took to keep him in the bouncer. We also did a-lot of slow introduction and building up of other playmates (we invited only one or two playmates over and supervised the bouncer in a much more controlled fashion). He still gets a bit dysfunctional with trying to pile all the other kids on top of him in the bouncer, but that has to do with his need for pressure which will be discussed next. But now he will go down the slide and run back into the bouncer to keep playing instead of simply bolting for the fields. This is a huge progression in socialization.

Something as basic as learning to play properly in a bouncer provides a number of therapies all at once. 1.) It builds – gross motor skills of balance and coordination. 2.) Helps develop close socialization and play skills with peers. 3.) Helps work out over stimulation issues with the rough and tumble environment. 4.) Gives the parents the opportunity to supervise proper play interaction. 5.) Helps develop his focus and toleration of other people in close quarters. 6.) The amount of people or playmates can be introduced in a controlled manner. As your child becomes accustomed to the play environment you can increase the amount of chaos (more playmates).

Again, setting up a controlled environment and going through rote mechanical (putting him back in a bouncer again and again – not letting him run away) repetition can have profound positive effects. Joy and fun can be taught, just like affection. I'll admit the hardest part was muscling through the pain of experiencing Emerson's dysfunctional behavior. In the beginning not one second of working him in the bouncer was fun. But with time it soon became a fun exercise in bonding. Jen and I would tumble on each other which would instigate Emerson to smile, run over and pile on us. Our family was coming together.

The Proprioceptive system: has to do with body awareness – the ability to sense pressure and physical surroundings. I mentioned this need in the upper paragraphs about the bouncer. Many autistic children find comfort in enclosed places. They pile couch cushions around them and have trouble focusing in wide open spaces. If your child has the need to bite, rough house, pushes kids constantly, keep putting himself in dark tight places (like in a box, under cushions, etc.) then understanding these needs are important.

So how do I use this to help my son listen when he bolts on the playground without having to exercise him through the "Stop and Go" therapy?

In wide open spaces your child has lost sense of his surroundings and becomes overwhelmingly excited. Getting him on the swings as soon as possible is one tactic. But he may still be too over stimulated to want to sit. Another tactic is to give him a little backpack weighted just enough to make him work at running. Children with Proprioceptive issues like having weight and pressure on them. They like the challenge of trying to run while weighted down. This also provides you the opportunity to keep up with them and even egg them on to keep going. (It's a great way to tire them out too).

Pressure vest: Another therapy is what's known as a pressure vest. It's a neoprene vest that is Velcro around the sides. This provides pressure and is supposed to have the same effect to calm them down. Another is "hug therapy." It sounds all warm and cuddly, but is used as a tool for when your child becomes too over stimulated say at a birthday party and becomes destructive. The parent picks the child up and firmly hugs to incapacitate him while leaving the room. I can't say this worked for Little Em. Removing him from the situation and putting him at task of stop and go had a much better effect.

Correcting self destructive behavior: Doctor Lovaas, the pioneer in developing Applied Behavioral Analysis, has a very distinct way of correcting self destructive behavior. He used to get the most severely afflicted children. For instance his facility received teenagers who spent the last decade of their lives chewing their fingers down a knuckle or who would perpetually bang their heads until bleeding. In an interview I have linked below, he discusses how these children came from other institutions or families that were unable to correct this behavior and were out of options. The parents inadvertently enabled the children to continually self inflict wounds because they simply didn't know how to handle such extreme behavior. However, Dr. Lovaas and his team tolerated none of this behavior. They didn't reason, they didn't coddle or ignore it hoping it would stop. They incited swift consequences for self destructive behavior. As a result, he professed the ability to correct children within days - or less.

To be politically correct I can't condone Dr. Lovaas technique of corporal punishment, but the best argument is in the results. I urge you to check out the entire article as it's utterly fascinating. Check out the link below to form your own opinion. http://www.neurodiversity. com/library_chance_1974.html

This is a hotly debated topic that rages on today. There are studies that profess both sides of the coin. Some studies show that children who receive corporal punishment have a higher rate of alcoholism, depression, anxiety and drug abuse later in life. Spanking or any other form of corporal punishment is banned in 28 states, however, still allowed in some private and public schools. Those who condone spanking say it actually decreases deviant behavior later in life and helps build a better citizen less likely to end up incarcerated.

The problem is this isn't just a debate of semantics – to spank or not to spank. The stakes are high. One of the gravest problems in using corporal punishment to correct behavior is it's easily escalated and abused. It comes to be relied upon instantly instead of a last resort.

Some may argue that the studies against corporal punishment are not dealing with autistic children. Dr. Lovaas used corporal punishment as a clinical tool that was used in combination with other regimented therapies along with a great amount of love and affection. As a matter of fact Lovaas professes punishment or discipline is not enough. "That our awareness of self is a product of love that we have received from others." This is where this book and Lovaas tie together. These exercises are forging to make our children aware of themselves and their surroundings, especially to the joys of family relationships.

By reading the results of Dr Lovaas, I find it hard to argue that corporal punishment was a greater evil than allowing a child to gnaw his fingers off. Lovaas employed extreme tactics under extreme circumstances. The main problem I see is a parent can interpret this as a green light to employ similar tactics to their child. As I mentioned it's so easy, especially for a frustrated emotional parent to unintentionally let it escalate to abuse, even lethal levels. Some statistics estimate anywhere from 1,000 to 2,000 children in the U.S. die every year from over-zealous corporal punishment every year. Furthermore, approximately 150,000 are seriously injured. This is obviously a slippery slope and something that has to be decided upon with all due care and monitored with calculating diligence.

Synopsis

Allowing temper tantrums and other destructive behavior will only fuel them to continue. Destructive and unacceptable behaviors must be dealt with in swift, consistent and divisive manner, but it must also be tempered, calculating and entwined with a great amount of love and affection. This is one of the most difficult aspects to balance and handle properly as a parent of an autistic child. The tactics in this chapter cannot be wrapped up in a paragraph or two. I suggest this chapter be read through whole if you find the need to make certain corrections for your child's tantrums. Lastly, look up the interview with Dr. Lovaas. He is the founder of ABA, the only therapy out there with statistical scientifically proven results. The article is quite an eye opener.

CHAPTER 11

BALANCE?

MAINTAINING THE ADULT RELATIONSHIP AND HOW MOMS AND DADS HANDLE THE STRESS OF PARENTING AUTISM DIFFERENTLY.

TRYING to derive some sense of life balance after being dealt the autism card is like trying to raise the white rhino sitting on the other end of the school ground seesaw. Let's get it out now. There is no balance and there will not be for the foreseeable future. Again, for most dads this is another trigger point to run as they stare down the double barrels of autism. Terrible things are going through your head. *The doctors can't give me any real prognosis of when or how my son will or won't come out of this. If I'm never going to have the son I thought I would and if I can't enjoy my wife as I used to, then what's the point of staying in the game?*

I remember one father confessing to me under his breath. "My son bangs his head to the point he bleeds, he bites people who try to hold him. He's destroying our house, he spreads feces on the walls and we can't even go out in public for fear of what he might do." He looked deep into my eyes as he finished with beaten conviction. "My life is a nightmare."

"I know what you mean," I whispered back. "I feel like that song from The Talking Heads." I quoted *Once in A lifetime*: 'This is not my beautiful house, this is not my beautiful wife, and I ask myself… Well, how did I get here?'

"Exactly," he chuckled.

"Hang in there," I said. "You're not the only one living in the Twilight Zone."

You have to apply some irony or comedy to your situation at any point possible. Levity can be the great glue to not only bring, but hold people together. Unfortunately, the relationship between husband and wife at this point has seen its way far beyond that. The fine china of marriage isn't simply broken on the floor, its being put through a blender.

I remember coming home that day and quoted the same line from the song to my wife. My attempt at humor laid dead and unnerved her. "So what are you trying to say, are you leaving?"

It was the last thing I was trying to do, but maybe she knew me better than I knew myself. My point, seeing the marriage through all the problematic nuances of autism is going to take much more than some light hearted comments or a buck-up-and-hang-in-there pat on the back from any therapist or book you read. It will take a super-human effort from both parties. You must come to grips that you are ordinary people being put through extraordinary stress. My best advice is approach your marriage and relationship with the same disciplined therapeutic mindset that you approach your child's situation.

This may sound a bit drastic, but the husband and wife relationship can get swallowed whole within days. First, you get the diagnosis and both of you recede to your corners to internally cope. Remorse, anger, despair and any compilation thereof take over. After the initial shock, the overwhelming learning curve takes precedence. The immersion of therapists, books and theories fill every space of your mind and soul. You begin to understand why you can't go out to public places, you recede from your friends or they recede from you. And before you know it, three, six or twelve months go by and you can't recollect the last time you had a quality adult night with each other.

Women are much better at postponing the adult relationship and still maintain that 'everything will be alright' when they eventually get back to it – whenever that is – sometime later – long down the road. As I notated earlier, they become 'Mama Bears' and as far as Mom is concerned, Papa Bear can wait in the wings as long as it takes. The "Balance" described in this chapter is not just in spending time together as adults, but just as importantly pertains to each other's parental duties with the child. It's why the chapter *Get Involved* was placed so early in the book for dads. It helps minimize the above scenario and leave the emotional doors open so mom will *want* to spend quality time together. If your wife doesn't feel like you have been working as hard in your own way then your want of an adult night just conveys as selfishness and builds further resentment.

Plan Events: As disciplined and regimented as your therapy has become for your child, it is a good idea to do the same for the two of you. It gives you something to look forward to. Your adult relationship needs therapy and intervention just as your child does. I know it couldn't sound any less romantic or spontaneous, but let's face the facts. That went out the window when your child's diagnosis crashed the room. Like everything else in your life, to save your sanity you will have to be as pragmatic and disciplined about your adult time.

Mom, it's easy to be dismissive and minimize the relationship with your husband. You're exhausted, distracted and consumed by your child's condition. But step back and realize your adult relationship is an imperative cog in the complicated mechanics of your child's therapy.

So imagine you finally get to spend a night out on your own together. Your wife is looking forward to talking the situation out and get reassurance that everything will work out while the husband was looking forward to a night of trying to forget and relax just for a bit. Here's where a man and woman's inner survival mechanisms can work against each other. As a blessing and curse men are much better at compartmentalizing. We are better able to put autism in a box, just for a couple hours in the hopes of having a true mental vacation.

I believe it's a coping mechanism from the hunter gatherer days. Compartmentalization allowed us to stay sharp and focused while at the task at hand like hunting dangerous game. Not being distracted with inner turmoil gave us a much better chance at catching game while not getting killed or eaten in the process. But this juxtaposed styles of dealing with this situation is a volatile cocktail that can not only ruin a night, but the entire marriage.

This may be a familiar scenario. After finally making the leap to trust a babysitter or family member with your child the two of you finally go out for a couple of drinks on a Friday night. The husband views this as a complete breakthrough and wants to be with his wife as he did before the baby, hold her with lust in his eyes, make innuendo's for later while mommy is still consumed with inner turmoil and is a bit unnerved with her husband's ability to just "forget" about their issues awaiting them at home. She starts to talk about their child's most recent disturbing stim or other atypical behavior. The husband pulls away frustrated, sighs and takes a heavy swig of his stiff drink as the wife interprets his behavior as uncaring for their child. He sees her as unable to take just a couple hours to let go and enjoy herself and the night begins its downward spiral. The good intentions of an adult night out can easily cause more damage than good if self awareness and compassion aren't ever-present.

No one is right or wrong here. There are just two different ways in which men and women handle this stressful situation. Once this is understood and accepted by both parties it can be called out and worked around.

Just because the husband can compartmentalize easier doesn't mean he doesn't love his child any less. And imagine how frustrating it must be for your husband? Try to imagine going away on vacation and your husband sat on the beach with his lap top and kept in constant contact with work. You bring him a drink to ease him off the computer and start to talk about how gorgeous the island is, but every conversation gets spun back round to work. I imagine it would become frustrating in quick fashion. A vacation is time to forget and recharge and so should a night out from autism. Though we have to be realistic in not being able to completely forget the situation at home, the point of adult night is to regroup, relax and try to ease the mental dismay.

Make the compromise. Trying to say your child's issues will not be discussed during the adult night out is simply unreasonable dad. But try to make the decision that it will be discussed only to a limit and that it must be in a positive fashion. Give each other the out to call a conversation to a stop if it starts to get upsetting.

The best way to help your child is if your adult relationship is intact. As much as it may seem like one of the chores and as tired as you are, getting out in public, meeting with adult friends can be a recharge. Sit back, take a sip of wine and try to swallow some solace that together, all that you are doing will work out for the best. You may be surprised how much a little squeeze and smile from your spouse can melt away the weight from your shoulders.

Don't expect anyone else to truly understand — even family members.

I have to put this subject somewhere in the book and I feel this is about the best place for it. Trying to lean on anyone other than your husband or wife for true understanding will most likely lead to disappointment. If you lean too hard you're likely to fall flat on your face. I remember someone professing this to us but we didn't really understand until one night Jen and I were discussing to a family member about all we were enduring over the phone about the uncertainty of the upcoming IEP meeting, the combined cost of daycare, Early Intervention, the attorney's fees and all the co-pays running us thousands of dollars a month. How we were perpetually worried about him wandering out of the house on a freezing night and would he ever really come out of his thousand mile stare.

"Well don't dwell on it." We were told.

"Wha?" We were speechless. This is where I realized most people outside our situation simply couldn't handle or truly understand what we were enduring. This is also when I realized from now on it simply wasn't healthy to carry on in any detail about what was going on in our lives. There's simply no way for people to understand what you're living through every sixty seconds of every minute, every sixty minutes of every hour, every twenty four hours a day, seven days a week for fifty two weeks a year… "Don't dwell on it?"

The family member realized we were incensed and threw out the statement, "leave it to God" as some sort of defense tactic to keep me from reaching through the phone and strangling them. What that family member didn't realize was if I was to hear one more person say in a song like fashion, "God only gives you what you can handle," I seriously contemplated tearing one of their limbs off and beating them with it.

Jen and I got off the phone in a rather short manner before losing our cool. From that point on we both made the point to keep much of our dismay to ourselves. It was this point as well that we realized we really needed each other in order to make it through with any sanity.

IT'S HARD NOT TO BLAME GOD.

Religion can be a great base to draw strength and if you have faith, more power to you. I envy you in a way. Not that I am an atheist, I'm the product of the Protestant Ethic. My basis of control and strength comes from within. I never grew up being told things were 'God's will' and I take offense to those who believe that all that comes upon us is His will. I think it's naïve and a surrendering cop-out statement to all that goes wrong in our lives and opens up God to take the blame for bad things that happen to us. I know it did for me. The meltdown of everything around me into the world of autism made me even more distant and angry with any belief that God had some greater design for this horrible condition. How can autism and possible retardation of my son be God's will?

The irony is, the more I educated myself on the causes of autism the more I realized my son's condition truly has nothing to do with God's will. Society's irresponsible actions on a whole have assaulted the natural order of things for generations. As I discuss the causes of autism in the next chapter it becomes quite apparent this condition is manmade. The devil is in our negligence, greed and arrogance. The poison we have discarded into the finite skies and injected into our infants is now settling in the aquifer of our population. And now the most sensitive, our children, are rising to the surface with disturbing conditions. Worse yet, with the new understanding of epigenetics discussed in the next chapter, it will take generations to dredge these poisons from our gene pool. This was never God's will.

I guess what I'm getting at here is it's hard not to lash out and look for blame, ask "why me" to a greater power. But God isn't "only giving you what you can handle" and he isn't to blame. We did this to ourselves. He's simply there to lean on if you can find Him.

CHAPTER 12

CANARIES IN A COAL MINE

or Three Legged Frogs in a Dirty Pond? Discussing Autism's Causes, The Holes Behind Each Theory and The New Science That May Finally Be Up to the Task of Pinning Down The Culprits.

THIS chapter may be of particular interest as I delve deeper and confront many of the loose ends and inconsistencies in each theory behind autism's causes. Finally I discuss a new science that may be up to the task of tying all these loose ends in a pretty bow.

I know this may seem as though it has little to do with strategies toward bonding parents to their children, but I am looking to spare you the countless hours of hunting the web for answers. Personally, I found myself investigating to the point of distraction. In fact it became quite an unhealthy obsession of sorts. Hours that I could have spent interacting with my son I spent instead in front of a computer screen in search of **The Answer**. My work was suffering and my relationship with Jen waned even further as I would inundate her with facts and statistics night after night.

However, finding the reasons for Emerson's condition has finally helped me deal with his problematic behaviors with more compassion and empathy than I ever could have before obtaining this knowledge.

It has also put to rest some of the burning questions I know we all have and allowed me to move forward in helping Emerson on a daily basis.

Autistic children have been compared to 'canaries-in-a-coal-mine' by some scientists. What an apt term. Canaries were the oversensitive indicators of unseen and odorless deadly gases in coal mines. It's also a coincidence that the term is inexplicably tied to the hazards of coal mining as evidence is mounting that the third most poisonous heavy metal (mercury) pumped by the ton into our skies from coal burning power plants is tied to autism. But today I feel the term 'canary-in-a-coal-mine' no longer applies. At this point the 'three legged frogs in a dirty pond' is more painfully accurate. This term refers to the alarming increase of deformed frogs being discovered in polluted ponds. I know this sounds horrific, but our children's minds are being deformed before our eyes in similar fashion.

So, why is my son autistic? Why wasn't there such a diagnosis for autism until the 1940's – about ten years after the first thimerosal laced vaccines? Why back in the 70's was 1 in 10,000 diagnosed with an ASD and now it's 1 in 150? Worse yet, if it's a boy odds are now 1 on 94! Why do older men and women have a higher incidence of bearing autistic children? Why is autism still rising even after thimerosal has either been completely removed or relegated to trace amounts in our children's vaccines? Why are some children showing autistic signs after vaccination while others show signs before vaccinations? How could autism be linked to genetics when it's spreading more like a plague? Why is the North East, specifically New Jersey ranked highest in the nation for ASD diagnosis?

Finding answers to these questions is of course a monumental if not a seemingly impossible task. Great minds have been at work on this for decades and I believe all the scientists are on the right track, but there always seems to be loose ends swinging in the breeze. For instance, take the thimerosal theory; that the ethylmercury based preservative/antibacterial is to blame for the exponential rise in autism. Its foundation is that the number of required vaccines increased in the eighties and nineties raised the levels of ethylmercury directly injected into our children to toxic levels. Indeed, in the 1930's there were only about three vaccines required. The current vaccine schedule is now up to around 25 by the first 18 months of life. The cumulative exposure to thimerosal was completely overlooked as the number of vaccinations increased. There is strong documentation to support this theory, but the lose end - the Achilles heel, is if this were the only answer then how come many children are born with the symptoms before ever being vaccinated? Furthermore, in 2000 the CDC agreed to the removal of thimerosal from infant vaccines 'as a precaution' even though they found 'no causal relationship' and the decline in thimerosal laced vaccines began in 2001. So why is the incidence of autism in children still increasing after thimerosal has either been removed or reduced down to trace levels in the vaccine regimen? One would imagine there would at least be a leveling off if not a great decrease in diagnosed newborns.

The focus then seemed to shift toward genetics. This was even one of the explanations the CDC used in defending against the thimerosal theory. Undeniably, there are an increasing number of "suspect" genes that have been identified in connection with autism. It has also been documented that autism has a heredity factor. If one child is diagnosed, the propensity of the parents having another child with the condition is greatly increased. But a simple answer of genetic mutation is flawed and utterly incomplete as well. Autism has shown a correlation to older fathers, the belief that somehow our gene pool is slowly breaking down as we age but once again this is incomplete. There are plenty of cases of young parents who sire autistic children. What about the cases of identical twins where one is normal and the other autistic? Researchers have proven their entire DNA to be absolutely identical, so how can one child be afflicted with autism and the other not? (Hint, epigenetics). Furthermore, if autism were only genetic then how can hard gene mutations take place over entire populations in a matter of two or three generations? The answer is it's impossible. True wide spread hard genetic mutation is caused either by slow glacier like evolution or a grave environmental cataclysm like nuclear war. We all can't trace our lineage back to the same family some eighty years ago and identify the errant gene that has carried through the generations and there hasn't been an environmental cataclysm like nuclear war – or has there? Furthermore, we're not dealing with something like fragile X or Downs's syndrome; conditions that are irreversible due to their hard gene maladies. Autism has been proven malleable, even reversible in some cases. If autism was a true hard gene mutation, reversing the condition would be like curing a person from Down's Syndrome.

You may see articles hinting that scientist are getting closer to identifying which genes are "causing autism." They are finding genes aren't "broken" but just "not expressed properly, (this is the core of epigenetics explained further down). But saying these misfiring genes are the "cause of autism" is missing the mark. It's like scientists finding the misfiring genes in the three legged frogs and saying it's due to "chromosome 34 being improperly expressed". No, they don't have three legs because chromosome 34 malfunctioned, it's because they were sired in a toxic soup that's causing chromosome 34 to misfire. In the past everyone suspected the polluted pond, but couldn't prove "evidence of harm or causal relationship" between the poison in the pond and the three legged frogs, but that's all about to change. What many people don't realize is epigenetics is now revealing how these suspect chemicals improperly express genes even down a multigenerational level - but I'm getting ahead of myself here.

Some blame pollution. A recent study in California illustrated the incidence of autism increased up to six fold in children born within closer proximity to fields sprayed with pesticides. Another study regarding environmental mercury release by coal burning power plants and its correlation to increased autism diagnosis in Texas has just been released as well. One table shows a 60% increase in children diagnosed with ASD with every additional 1,000 pounds of mercury belched in to the air by coal burning power plants. Again, big corporations that produce these chemicals and even the government look at these numbers as circumstantial and indeed finding the bridge to tie evidence of harm to these compounds has been elusive.

All these hints and clues have frustrated parents and dragged researchers in different directions in a panicked search for **The Answer**. Everyone wants to find the single smoking gun, hold it in the air for all to morbidly marvel and sneer at before locking it away so it can never hurt our children again. Scientists and parents are frantically trying to prove 'the causal relationship' so we can once and for all pin the culprit down to make the necessary changes.

I think the answers are already here in front of us. We just need to step back and look at the environmental changes that have taken place over the last eighty years and open our minds to the relatively new science of epigenetics. Epi is a prefix taken from the Greek language meaning "near or on." Epigenetics is revolutionizing our understanding of genetics, the environment and the way they interact with one another. And for the first time I believe we have a science that is up to the task of explaining the complexities of autism's causes – and I do mean that in the plural sense. It will tie a pretty little bow around all the above theories loose ends and to our horror prove everyone right. The reason I say 'horror' is because if the factors causing this disorder aren't addressed systematically and comprehensively, the prognosis is grim. I know this may sound odd, but it would be a Godsend to prove that just thimerosal was the problem. We could remove it as we have and move on. But this disaster is grotesquely bigger than thimerosal. Epigenetics explains why older parents are more likely to conceive autistic children and how adults exposed even subtly to substances like pesticides, thimerosal laced vaccines and heavy metal discharge over a lifetime can affect their offspring who were never directly exposed to these chemicals for generations to come. But before going into this, let's look into some of the things that we do know are affecting our children today and then how the new science ties autism's causes together.

I kept hearing the thimerosal theory chirping in my ear, the correlation to mercury poisoning and thimerosal laced vaccines, but

I really knew very little about it. Many studies are quite compelling when tying together the symptoms, but I had originally dismissed the thimerosal theory because Emerson was born in 2005 and the pediatrician assured us his vaccinations were mercury free. The antibacterial preservative had either been removed or relegated to trace amounts in his vaccines. Furthermore, my son seemed to show signs of autism right from birth. But something has to be a culprit, right? I had to start somewhere when it came to narrowing down all the 'whys'.

So I looked back to the time before there was autism, vaccinations, and many other things our wonderful world of technology and industrialization now has to offer. In 1796, British doctor Edward Jenner made the observation that milkmaids who contracted the harmless cowpox virus never contracted smallpox. Though smallpox was sometimes fatal, Jenner somehow justified an experiment on an eight year old boy in which he purposefully infected with the cowpox virus by scratching his arm with puss taken from an infected milkmaid. Sure enough, little James Phipps contracted the innocuous cowpox. Six weeks later Doctor Jenner scratched the puss from a small pox lesion in the boy's arm. To everyone's relief James showed no signs of illness or infection. (If this boy had a living mother, I have no idea how Jenner talked her into this.) In any event, the new procedure was called 'vaccination', (*vacca* is Latin for "cow") and it paved the way for the eradication of smallpox.

Fast forward to January 27, 1928. Twenty one children were injected with a vaccine against diphtheria. Within forty eight hours twelve were dead. An investigation revealed living staphylococci had tainted the vaccine.

Eli Lilly developed thimerosal in the 1920's; an antimicrobial/ antifungal that is 49.6% ethylmercury by weight and by 1930 testing began. They used 22 patients already dying of meningitis. They were injected and studied until their deaths, which was only a matter of days. It was declared that there were no observed side effects since they all died of their disease and not the injections. As a result thimerosal was added to vaccines and also introduced in over the counter remedies.

When the FDA was created, thimerosal was grandfathered into its approved medication list with no further testing. Obviously sound medicine was not being practiced here and as a result documented thimerosal poisonings took place. But before discussing thimerosal poisoning, there are two main types of mercury from which poisoning occurs.

Methylmercury: Inorganic mercury is pumped into our atmosphere from volcanoes, forest fires and the burning of fossil fuels, especially coal burning power plants. Methylmercury is formed when anaerobic organisms digest the inorganic mercury that is spewed into the atmosphere and settles in our lakes, rivers and oceans. The digestion converts inorganic mercury into the extremely poisonous organic methylmercury. The organic mercury bio-accumulates as it is passed up the food chain. As organisms consume other organisms, the heavy metal concentrations keep building – top level predator fish can be found to have a million times the amount of mercury in their flesh than the concentration found in polluted water. It has the ability to cross the blood brain barrier and pass through the placental wall to the developing fetus. Studies indicate that children exposed to methylmercury show loss of IQ points, developmental and speech delays, motor skill deficiencies, sensory problems, mental retardation and attention deficit disorders. According to the 2004 figures from the EPA, about 630,000 babies are born each year with dangerous levels of mercury in their blood.

Ethylmercury/Thimerosal: Unlike methylmercury, ethylmercury has not been found to bio-accumulate. Even though the side effects and toxicity levels of ethylmercury are not well known, exposure standards are based on methylmercury as recommended by the EPA. The view of the CHM remains that there is no evidence of adverse neurodevelopmental effects caused by thimerosal in vaccines. Even though there is documented evidence of thimerosal poisoning in the 1950's as you'll read below, the EPA and FDA are steadfast that the only evidence of harm due to thimerosal laced vaccinations is a small risk of hyper-sensitivity (that typically include skin rashes or local swelling at the site of injection). Their line of thinking is that thimerosal does not 'bio-accumulate' in our bodies, and that they only way ethylmercury becomes toxic is by 'prolonged or chronic exposure.' Well, aren't 25 repeated intramuscular injections over an 18 month period considered prolonged or chronic exposure? Studies showed the increased vaccina-tion schedule gravely increased the chronic level of mercury exposure well above the safety level determined by the EPA– something the FDA completely missed.

DOCUMENTED MERCURY POISONINGS, THEIR NAMES AND THEIR SYMPTOMS:

Acrodynia or Thimerosal poisoning: Also known as, Swifts, Feers or Pinks Disease: It was once very prevalent, but since the removal of thimerosal from over the counter remedies, it is now very rare. My understanding is in the 1950's thimerosal in infant's teething powders lead to fatalities. Symptoms would begin with irritability, tendencies to cry, loss of appetite, (all common when teething which made it diffi-cult to diagnose while parents kept administering the mercury laced medication). As the poisoning continues the conditions worsen with loss of muscle tone, atrophy, muscle pain, photophobia (sensitivity to light), pink flushing of hands, inattention, feet and cheeks that later turns a deeper reddish hue. Extreme pain and itchiness in the extremi-ties leads to thickening skin due to excessive scratching. Inflammation and erosion of gums can occur with possible loss of teeth. Hair and nail loss along with high probability of upper respiratory infections was also common. Profuse sweating can easily turn to prickly heat and secondary bacterial infections.

Curiously the symptoms were at times missed since the mercury could commonly be stored in the body to some extent, but as exposure continued intolerance would develop and symptoms would reveal themselves weeks after initial and continued administration. Also, not all children reacted similarly to exposure. It is hypothesized that some children may have developed latent allergic reactions or hypersensitivity because not all children contracted the disease.

There are some symptomatic comparisons to autism, but not as many as one would expect. The main tie I see here to autism is how some children were tolerant to thimerosal while others were much more sensitive and would develop latent intolerance or allergic like reactions with continued exposure. This is very interesting as this could correlate to the variances in the reaction to thimerosal laced vaccines from one child to the next. This is the only direct link or "evidence of harm" as the CDC likes to term it to thimerosal allergy/intolerance/poisoning and the documented varied severity from one child to another that I am aware of. As a result, thimerosal was removed from over the counter items in the 1950's, but oddly enough no one thought to remove it from our infant's vaccines.

As a side note it's obvious to me that, 'causal effect or evidence of harm' was determined for thimerosal as we can plainly see from the 1950's incidents. If this determination were applied to the vaccines today a windfall of lawsuits would be awarded, something the Government and pharma companies are obviously doing their best to quell. As a matter of fact a provision mysteriously slipped into the homeland Security Bill which passed in November 2002. The provision specifically protects Eli Lilly & Co and other pharma companies from lawsuits regarding thimerosal. It's my understanding that the provision was repealed in 2003 due to public outcry, but there's still a struggle for politicians to protect the pharma companies that have contributed to their campaigns.

Minimata disease: Named after the Japanese fishing town that was poisoned in the late 1950's and 1960's by industrial discharge of methylmercury into the Minimata Bay. Bioaccumulation in the fish led to an epidemic of mercury poisoning among the residents. Fetuses were found to be much more sensitive to the effects of methylmercury than adults who commonly showed no signs of poisoning. However when the infants were born, incidents of severe neurological damage resembling cerebral palsy erupted. Those exposed to lower levels while in-utero typically developed sensory, motor dysfunction, developmental delays and permanent loss of IQ points. There is also evidence that methylmercury exposure can cause autoimmune problems.

A similar accidental poisoning occurred in Basra Iraq in which grain destined for field planting was sprayed with mercury as an antifungal. The grain was stolen from the docks and sold on the black market. Though the grain was dyed red and marked poison, the warnings were ignored and consumed by people. The results were tragically similar to Minimata; loss of coordination, speech and hearing impairment and even death. Children exposed in-utero were affected with developmental delays, sensory issues and permanent mental retardation.

The Minimata and Basra incidents are confined and increasingly rare incidents now due to public awareness. What scientists are more concerned with are subtle effects of environmental methylmercury poisoning. As your read further, there are approximately 50 tons of methylmercury being industrially pumped into our skies on an annual basis in the United States alone. And personally, I see many similar symptoms in comparing autism to methylmercury poisoning.

OTHER WAYS IN WHICH MERCURY CAN POISON US AND OUR CHILDREN:

Handling mercury: Some parents today may remember holding mercury in their hands and curiously watching it roll about their palms. Mercury can poison through the skin, however, since mercury has a very low boil point (the temperature at which the liquid becomes a gas), the gases can be inadvertently inhaled as its being handled. The incidence of mercury poisoning from handling is now minimal since it has been removed from most over the counter thermometers. All old style thermometers and thermostats should be removed from the house hold.

Fluorescent light bulbs breaking: Okay fellas, how many out there have been involved in the breaking of florescent light tubes as a kid? I remember breaking them by a dumpster on the back parking lot as a stock boy for a local drug store. We thought the way they imploded was the coolest thing. Did anyone know they were releasing potentially toxic levels of mercury into the air? I didn't. There is a case in 1987 of a 23 month old child developing acute mercury poisoning to the point of near death. It was later discovered the child commonly played in the area where a case of florescent tubes previously broke and 'were cleaned up'.

It used to be that only the larger florescent tubes were the ones to worry about. They were rarely found in the house and were relegated to shops, offices or garages. But due to the emergence of the smaller energy efficient bulbs (CFL's – compact florescent light bulbs) they can now be found in most households. These small bulbs contain about 5 to 30 milligrams of mercury. I've read articles minimizing the risk of poisoning by reasoning that each bulb has about a hundred times less mercury than say a mercury thermometer, but what we're most concerned with is mercury vapor – the most viable route into our bodies other than injection. By the way, they fail to mention a broken mercury thermometer can contaminate a twenty acre lake to the point of making the fish inedible. Tests showed after the smaller Compact Florescent Light Bulbs were broken; the mercury vapor levels exceeded the Federal guidelines for chronic exposure by 100 times or more. (As a curious note, there's no set level by the Federal Government for acute exposure.) Even after several clean up techniques, the mercury levels still exceeded Federal guidelines. Of further concern, mercury vapors concentrate low to the ground. This makes infants more susceptible to inhale the vapor. The study concluded that certain precautions and techniques should be exercised if a bulb breaks. 1.) Children and pets should be removed from the area immediately. 2.) The house should be opened and well ventilated. 3.) A vacuum should never be used, and it's suggested that if the bulb is broken over carpeting, that the section should be cut out and removed. 4.) The cleaner's hands should be gloved and nothing touched with bare hands. 5.) The dust should be collected by a wet rag or tape and placed in a screw topped jar along with the broken bulb and glass shards.

For the articles that demote these bulbs internals to an innocuous side note, I sure find it curious that such drastic measures as cutting out a contaminated section of carpeting, using rubber gloves and toxic containment via a screw topped jar are deemed necessary for proper clean up. Worse yet, there are no warning labels on the packaging.

Coal burning power plants: There are approximately 1,100 coal burning power plants in the United States. Each year they pump out about 100,000 pounds of mercury into the atmosphere where it settles miles away and is converted into the highly toxic organic methylmercury in our lakes and streams. Most of the coal burning power plants are in the North East. In 2003, Pennsylvania had 36 coal-fired power plants that accounted for about 3.85 tons of mercury emitted into the air, ranking PA as second highest in the nation for mercury emissions. Now compare trade wind trajectories and it casts an ominous cloud over New Jersey, the state rated with the highest incidence of autism in the country. In New York State most of the fish are now unsafe to eat from mercury contamination and many of the Adirondack lakes are dead from acid rain. In Connecticut every freshwater fish is now unsafe to eat. The Fish and Wildlife Service announced that in 19 states it is unsafe to regularly eat any freshwater fish, and in 48 states at least some fish are unsafe to eat. The mercury is coming largely from those same 1,100 coal-burning power plants. Below is a recent study of environmental mercury release.

Environmental mercury release, special education rates, and autism disorder: an ecological study in Texas: You can type in the key words and find the document on the web. A recent study in

Texas examined the correlation of mercury released into the environment and rates of autism. Texas ranks fourth in the Nation among the highest in release of industrial mercury. The test correlated the percentage increase in the rate of autism for every 1,000 pounds of mercury released into the atmosphere as well as the families distance from the power plants. There are complicated tables and adjustments for demographics and distance, but the results were conclusive. In one model it showed a 63% increase in autism and in another model it showed a 43% increase in special education needs for every 1,000 pounds of mercury released. The model also correlated a decrease in ASD diagnosis the further away families were from coal burning power plants.

A March 2005 study by a group of pediatricians from the Mount Sinai Center for Children's Health entitled "Public Health and the Economic Consequences of Methylmercury Toxicity to the Developing Brain" stated that "the loss of IQ due to methylmercury affects between 10 and 15% of children born in America each year." Dr. Landrigan, director of the center said, "If mercury emissions are allowed to remain at these high levels children will continue to suffer loss in intelligence and disruptions of behavior."

Even-though we know mercury exposure can lead to lower intelligence, developmental delays, learning disabilities and behavioral problems there's still 'no causal effect' between the industrial release of mercury and autism, right? What the Federal Government and CDC will contest is when many children with autistic disorders are tested, they will fail to show elevated levels of mercury in their systems. This is where they lean back on their ropes of 'no causal effect' but once again recent experiments with epigenetics answers why that is.

As a side note, some argue that the Industrial Revolution surely would have greater amounts of mercury release. The coal soot skies of the industrial nations were historic as were the incidence of lung disease. Therefore, as one would imagine there should have been incidence of autism back then. Not a bad observation, however, some estimate that today there is approximately 5 times the amount of mercury pumped into the atmosphere than 150 years ago. And as we'll see, the effects of subtle mercury exposure may not build up and be discernable until generations later.

PESTICIDES:

Since my son showed autistic symptoms from birth, I first ignored the thimerosal theory and started with the symptoms associated with pesticide poisoning. I kept wondering if decades of exposure to minute amounts of pesticides over a couple generations finally built up enough in our systems to push our genetics off kilter, after all pesticides directly attack the nervous system. (And have you ever watched an insect hit with pesticide? I remember seeing some repetitively run a circle as their nervous system was being attacked.) I asked myself what else has been so pervasively spread across our lands other than fossil fuel emissions or thimerosal? For decades pesticides have been systematically spread across fields with little or no testing and little regard for its long term effects on humans. Take DDT for instance. Swiss Chemist Paul Meuler discovered its pesticide qualities and soon it was widely used in WWII to stem insects like mosquito's and lice. Incidents of malaria dropped from 75 million to 5 million within ten years. Meuler even won the Nobel Prize for his contribution to mankind and after the war farmers began using it for their fields. 1.2 billion pounds of DDT crept into streams and wells before the poison's collateral damage was realized. In 1962, Rachael Carson's book *Silent Spring* illustrated how DDT was killing birds and fish. It nearly wiped out the Bald Eagle, but still it took another decade of grass roots efforts by environmentalist and citizens before the Federal Government finally banned it. By the way, it's still produced in the United States and shipped for use overseas.

Take for instance the recent study below. Since pesticides have been around for over seventy years, I have no idea why it took so long for a study like this to take place. *Maternal Residence Near Agricultural Pesticide Applications and Autism Spectrum Disorders among Children in the California Central Valley:* This study released in July of 2007, tested the percentage of children diagnosed with ASD and their proximity to fields sprayed with organochlorine pesticide. The first study of its kind, they found the incidence of children born to ASD increased with the closer proximity and poundage of pesticide used in fields and decreased with increased distance from the fields. The conclusion is very much the same as the Texas study that correlates the increased release of methylmercury and the increased diagnosis of autism. Disturbingly, they found the incidence of ASD diagnosis increased up to six fold at the nearest points to the pesticide laced fields.

Here is another site that will lead you to many articles correlating environmental factors to autism. http://www.ravenintellections.com/autism-pollutants.htm

Pesticides and other chemicals of today seem to enjoy much of the same rights as a US citizen. That is, innocent until proven guilty beyond a shadow of a doubt. To my knowledge there are still no standardized long term tests to prove pesticide or chemical safety. Furthermore, the due process of proving a pesticide or chemical harmful by having 'direct causal effect to evidence of harm' is a tedious long procedure that allows for damage to continue on human beings while testing is conducted. There are approximately 7,000 new chemicals introduced into the market every year, yet only one or two taken off. Take BPA, the chemical leached from clear plastic bottles when they are heated up. This is of particular concern when it comes to the hard plastic baby bottles that are heated in the microwave. Studies on animals show changes in behavior and the brain, increased risk of certain cancers and early onset of puberty. Yet the government hasn't requested the removal of the chemical. Instead, as news got around and consumers became concerned our retailers took on the job of making the decision to discontinue selling products with BPA. By the way, Canada already banned BPA's production and sale in their country.

SO WHICH IS IT?

It is pesticides, methylmercury, thimerosal or other chemicals? The answer: Yes, it's every one of those things - and more. The government has been unable to find a 'direct causal link' to these compounds and autism because many times blood work of the afflicted child does not show elevated levels of the suspect compounds. So, how can we tie this all together and show our politicians who need "causal relation" that these things are indeed destroying our children's minds? How do we prove that subtle poisoning over generations is finally pushing our genetic material to its limits when our hard DNA strands show no changes? Where is the bridge to lead everyone to evidence of harm?

Enter the new science of epigenetics. Our understanding of static genetics, biology, the environment and how they interact is quickly changing. Epigenetic science is proving to be the very bridge we are looking for. In 2001 the mapping of the human genome was thought to solve all of life's mysteries. Scientists imagined once they had the book of life, they could then compare disease to genetic codes – change the codes back to where they belonged and cure it. But they soon discovered that disease still reared its head without any gene mutation. It was particularly evident in identical twins developing profoundly different diseases. Schizophrenia, autism or cancer would afflict one twin while the other was unaffected. This left the scientists scratching their heads after their genetic codes were proven identical. So what was going on?

When you think about the fact that most cells in your body carry your full genetic code, how do your skin cells know to only become more skin cells? What's programming them to only use (or express) the genes needed to create and maintain that cell? Triggers outside the entire gene strand that express or suppress their programming have been discovered. The gene's expression is known as methylation. This is the cornerstone of epigenetic science. It's a tough concept, but I think of it like this. Imagine a grand piano as a cell. Each key on the piano represents a single gene on the DNA strand. Each key (or gene) is designed to express a specific note if triggered or make no sound if untouched or suppressed. Now imagine a pianist sitting before the keyboard – he is the epigenetic expresser. He begins to play a beautiful song, hitting each key (or gene) releasing its code. He composes a perfect melodic body of sound. He can even play the keys soft to partially express the gene. One set of keys expressed in a certain order create a skin cell. Another set of keys played represent nerve cells. One can close their eyes to the beauty as the soothing cacophony of notes gel in perfect unison to make a whole. But then the Pianist (or epigenetic trigger) gets disturbed by a fly buzzing around his ear or a cough from the audience (the environment) and he hits the wrong key (or expresses the wrong gene.) The wrong note rings sour changing the entire melody or in this case, cause a nerve cell to not form and function properly. The body of music or physical nerve cell is no longer in tune.

A gene mutation would be equated to a broken piano key or snapped wire. What has been so elusive to scientists is that the piano keys (or genes) were not damaged, making it impossible to explain why things were going wrong. What they realize now is errors in gene programming can cause as dramatic and cataclysmic physical problems in the body as hard gene mutation.

So what has changed that could cause our genetic programming to run awry at such an exponential rate? What's changed over the last thirty or forty years to cause the diagnosis of ASD to go up 1,500%? What scientists are proving is the epigenome system is much more sensitive to environmental factors than the hard genes. Even though the genes aren't mutated, profound adverse affects can still occur not only on the individual, but to our dismay, can also effect many future generations down the line. Like bioaccumulation occurs with methylmercury it has been discovered that epigenetic accumulation occurs as well. Over a person's life time, environmental factors alter our epigenetic programming. What's worse yet is some of these mutations can be passed down to future generations. For instance, Michael Skinner, a professor of molecular biosciences and director of the Center for

Reproductive Biology at Washington State University, and his team described in the 3 June 2005 issue of *Science* how they briefly exposed pregnant rats to the insecticide methoxychlor and the fungicide vinclozolin, and documented the ill effects. The increased cancer and neurological disorders were documented in about 85% of the mice. The mice were checked for any gene damage and there was none. I repeat – no hard genetic damage.

Here's the most frightening discovery. As the mice were bred from the original parents, the percentage of offspring affected with the same ailments continued at the same rate four generations later. **Even though there was no genetic damage or direct contact with pesticide, the offspring four generations down the line behaved as if they had been directly poisoned.** Digging for more information, they found altered DNA methylation of certain genes. (Now correlate this finding to our exposure to pesticides, thimerosal and methylmercury over the last few generations and you can see why it's been so hard to find 'direct causal effect'.) The scientists call this genomic imprinting, but I think that's an incomplete term. It doesn't specify what epigenetic triggers are passed down to our descendants and expressed. Not all epigenetic changes are passed down and expressed through later generations, as illustrated with twins where one is autistic and one is typical. Even though they have identical genes passed down by the same parents, the epigenetic mutations are expressed in one and not the other. I think a more comprehensive term would be 'parental epigenetic mutation expressed in descendants', or PEMEID. The environmentally altered epigenetic code from the parent is passed down and incorrectly triggers the genes to behave as if the neurotoxin was directly present. Indeed, much of the research today illustrates the genetic anomalies associated with autism are improper methylation or expression. In other words the genetic anomalies associated with autism are for the most part epigenetic. This helps explain why trying to find the 'damaged gene's' has been so elusive to scientist. The genes are not broken; they're simply the victim of improper expression or suppression.

The thing I find disturbing is the media seems to sensationalize how scientists are discovering what genes are involved in autism. They feebly describe gene expression, but no one seems to be asking the question "Why is there such a jump in improper gene programming? What is happening to cause all these epigenetic mutations?"

Epigenetics ties together the elusive gap of "causal relationship" of methylmercury, thimerosal and pesticides when it comes to connecting it to our children. As this and other startling experiments illustrate that epigenetic changes may endure for at least four subsequent generations presents the argument that so long as thimerosal laced flu vaccines are pumped into our bodies in adulthood, each vaccination chips away at our epigenetic programming. (Thimerosal has only been removed from infant vaccinations – it's still laced in our adult flu shots). The older we get the more damage our epigenetic code endures and the greater chance we have at passing down maladies that will profoundly affect a newborn even though he or she has never been directly exposed to the toxins.

Our sheet music of life is naturally altered as we grow older; however, compounds like thimerosal, pesticides and methylmercury are shredding it beyond repair. 'Parental epigenetic mutation expressed in descendants' is a new concept, but nevertheless a very real factor that needs to be added to the equation of environmental pollution and its causal effects when being presented to government officials.

Further studies have found epigenetic alterations occurring over the full course of a human life span. In the 2005 July issue of *Proceedings of the National Academy of Sciences,* Manel Esteller, director of the Cancer Epigenetics Laboratory at the Spanish National Cancer Center in Madrid evaluated 40 pairs of twins from 3 to 74 years of age. They found younger twins had nearly identical DNA epigenetic patterns. If the similarities were to be highlighted as yellow, the two sets superimposed on each other look nearly the same. However, older twins, especially those with different lifestyles had vastly different patterns from one another. This helps explain why one twin gets cancer while the other doesn't.

Epigenetic codes are designed to be malleable to allow an organism's quick adaptation for survival over only a generation or two so it can survive rapid environmental changes. What nature hasn't prepared for is the curveball of manmade neurotoxins in our environment. The terrifying specter this raises is these elements are wreaking havoc not only on us, but on our children and possibly for generations to come.

Epigenetic science provides the only comprehensive picture that ties together many of the 'loose ends' that the separate theories of autism could not answer:

1.) *Why it has it been so difficult for scientist to pin down the genes that cause autism?* The genes have not mutated, therefore the scientist are missing what's really happening. Only when they looked into gene methylation did they start to see many 'hot spots' correlating to autism. See article: Epigenetics of autism spectrum disorders: (HumanMolecularGenetics200615(Revi ewIssue2):R138R150;doi:10.1093/hmg/ddl213)http://hmg. oxfordjournals.org/cgi/reprint/15/suppl_2/R138

2.) *Why are some children 'born' with autistic symptoms before being vaccinated?* The damaged epigenetic code inherited from the parents is expressed in a newborn.

3.) *Why are children born with neurological disorders, yet don't show elevated levels of mercury or pesticides in their system?* Their epigenetic code was already altered before they were born. This is perhaps the most profound bridge that has eluded proponents of thimerosal and other poisons from proving causal relationship. No one knew these heavy metals and other toxins could leave DNA intact, yet still wreak havoc down a multigenerational level as proven with recent experiments.

4.) *Why are older couples more prone to sire autistic children?* The longer we live, the more our epigenetic code is assaulted by adult thimerosal laced flu shots, pesticides, methylmercury, smoke and all the other every day environmental hazards of life. Furthermore, this presents an excellent argument to rid ALL vaccines of thimerosal. Even though our adult bodies can tolerate thimerosal in flu vaccines and such, we are damaging our epigenetic code for our future generations.

5.) *Why do some children respond to Chelation even when their bodies don't show any high levels of heavy metals?* Their inherited epigenetic systems are making their bodies behave as if they are being poisoned even though it may not be physically in their system. Chelation may stimulate methylation of the epigenetic system to respond as if the ghost toxins have been removed. (This has yet to be proven, but it would be interesting to compare gene expression before and after Chelation.) This may sound like a stretch, however, it has already been proven that something as simple as affection or neglect can alter the epigenetic expression and actually permanently change body chemistry in offspring. This will be discussed in the next chapter.

6.) Epigenetic science may also relate as to why some children have a hyper reaction to thimerosal laced vaccines when injected. As we see with the thimerosal poisonings in the 1950's, some children had much less toleration than others after prolonged exposure.

There may be some questions that I'll try to answer: *If epigenetics is true, is there research to being done to reprogram epigenetic malfunctions?* Yes, as a matter of fact there is and it mostly is in the realm of cancer research. In essence epigenetic therapy is to not kill the cancer cells, but to be more subtle. The idea is to correct the expression or suppression of the genes to get the cancer cells to behave as they were originally programmed. To say, 'hey you're not a cancer cell,' and remind it to be the lung cell it was supposed to be. This is wonderful for the treatment of cancer because it would spare the person the poisonous remedy and horrendous side effects of chemotherapy.

Is there any success in this research? Yes. It is very preliminary, but there are tests with some very positive results. Take MDS, cancer of the blood and bone marrow. It is a type of leukemia. There was no known cure and people diagnosed with the disease were typically given only a few months to live. An experimental drug was administered with the idea to correct the epigenetic expression of tumor suppressing genes. It was believed that over the course of life that the tumor suppressor gene was accidentally turned off or suppressed. The drug was designed to turn it back on. In nearly 50% of the patients the disease completely disappeared after administering the drug. This is an immense break though since previous mortality rates were 100%. It's obvious that epigenetic science is not simply theory or conjecture. It is working science.

Is there any research looking to correct the improper DNA methylation in autistic children? To me, the problem with taking this approach towards "curing" autism is trying to do it the hard way. As we are seeing, autism has an infinite amount of variables in how individuals are affected. And as scientists delve deeper into discovering which genes are improperly expressed, they're finding this task to be laced with infinite variables. These compounds mixed and exposed to us in variable amounts on something so complicated as our epigenetic system has the propensity for an infinite amount of epigenetic mutations. Trying to find every single malady and individually chemically repair it is a road we've been forced to take, but it's ass backwards. I have an idea, let's take a stronger approach to not expose ourselves to the chemicals in the first place. Scientist can try to chemically fix the three legged frogs in the polluted pond, but we're still going to keep getting deformed frogs so long as they're still swimming in a toxic soup. Once we prove causal relationship to certain chemicals and autism we can begin to really get to the heart of stopping it by cleaning up the chemicals that are causing it in the first place.

I would like to share an email I sent to Dr. Michael Skinner, the Principal Investigator and professor in the School of Molecular Biosciences at Washington State University. His work is on the forefront of epigenetic research and has been highlighted in the PBS documentary *Ghost In Your Genes* and in 2005 and 2007 was selected within the top 100 discoveries by Discover.

My email Subject is titled: *Epigenetic expression comparison in identical twins where one is autistic and other is developing normally.*

Hello Dr. Skinner,

My name is Emerson Donnell and I am the father of an autistic child. I am fascinated with your research regarding epigenetics and believe we finally have a science that is up to the task of tying together the causes of autism. I do believe environmental insults like pesticides, thimerosal and mercury to the population over the last few generations have finally stretched our genetics past their limits. As you know, the big problem is showing causal relationship since the chemicals affecting some children aren't directly in the body, but perhaps their epigenetic code was altered by exposure to these chemicals generations earlier. In the Nova program Ghost in your Genes, there is a case of identical twins where one is normally developing while the other is severely autistic. I understand their gene or DNA sequence is identical and that the problem points towards improper gene expression. Would you be able to compare their epigenetic expression codes as well and then determine (hot spot) epigenetic areas that might be associated with autism? If you test enough sets of twins there may be some real common areas to help scientists focus on.

On another note of causal relationship of autism and thimerosal:

You may also be able to affect rats with thimerosal, compare their epigenetic expression prior to and after exposure and even breed them to see if the epigenetic mutations carry down as they did with your experiment with pesticides. You can also compare any neurological impairments that may occur. Furthermore, if these epigenetic mutations coincide with the epigenetic 'hot spots' discovered on autistic children (in your twins comparison) there may finally be the "Causal Effect" that has been so elusive to tying

*autism to environmental factors. I understand your a very busy
professional and don't mean to bother you. But by being able to
now see before and after effects chemicals can have on gene expression - as well as generations down the line, it seems like there is a
great opportunity available in the few sets of twins out there with
this situation. If the hot spots can be identified, perhaps treatments can be created to properly express the troubled genes.*

*Thank you so much for taking the time to listen to my thoughts.
If you have any inclination to reply I would extremely excited
to hear your position. I think your research will one day change
everyone's understanding of our genetics, the environment and
just how fragile we all really are.*

*All The Best,
Emerson*

I was very excited to get a reply from Dr. Skinner who as a scientist, lead investigator and university professor is obviously quite a busy
person. Below is his response.

*Dear Mr. Donnell,
Thank you for the email and interest in our research. You are
right the environmental factors affecting the epigenome will be a
factor in many disease states including autism. We are mapping
the epigenome in our model to provide proof of the concept we
can identify epigenetic biomarkers and correlate this to disease
and exposure. However, the difference in species is dramatic
in the epigenome, in contrast to the genome sequence of DNA.
Therefore, the markers identified in rats will likely be different
in humans. However, with time cohorts of patients, such as
autism patients and families, can be used to map the potential
epigenetic biomarkers or 'hot spots' in humans disease. This will*

require some new technology and time, but we are moving in that direction. So yes your idea of mapping twins, and general cohorts of control versus disease patient will be useful in the future. In regards to what compounds may promote specific disease, this will also take time, and if we have the epigenetic biomarkers we can then monitor exposure and differences for different compounds. So hopefully this new area of epigenetics will facilitate our understanding of how disease develops and how we can eventually treat it more effectively.

Thank you again for the interest in the research and your comments.

Cheers,

Michael Skinner

With great minds like Dr. Skinner's on the case it looks like help is on the way, however, my guess is it won't be for some time.

SO IS ANY AMOUNT OF TOXIC EXPOSURE SAFE?

The Federal Government has standardized what it perceives as a 'tolerable or safe level' of mercury and pesticide exposure, but at the time they had no understanding of epigenetic accumulation, environmentally induced epigenetic alterations nor how parental epigenetic mutation can be passed down to children. The revelations in epigenetic science illustrates there will never be a safe or tolerable level of these toxins.

Methylmercury, pesticides, and thimerosal are much like the deadly gases in the coal mines. They're silent, odorless and invisible – especially when their effects are epigenetically passed down to our children. They have insidiously poisoned the minds of our helpless children without leaving behind a telltale trail of genetic mutations or toxic chemical/heavy metal signatures that everyone was looking for.

The causal relation of these neurotoxins to autism has been elusive, but our eyes are now open, at least for some.

I will end this chapter as a personal plea to the powers that be to sit up, take notice and make changes as quickly as possible. I appeal directly to The President, Congress, The Center for Disease Control and The Environmental Protection Agency. These individuals and agencies can institute immediate change. But instead they wait for parents and privately funded scientists to find "causal relationships to autism" as the damage continues to accumulate and rip deeper into our social and genetic fabric. My hope is that the incestuous relationship between politicians and industry will be set aside and common sense will prevail. (I can hear the sardonic snickers from the last statement.) I know this is a pipe dream, and regretfully environmental corrections won't be placed on the forefront. That is until our politician's offspring or grandchildren are afflicted, and unfortunately at this rate it is inevitable. Only then, when they try to fruitlessly look into the distant eyes of their own children and pray for them to come back to our world will the wheels of change truly begin to turn.

This is a manmade catastrophe and only man can turn this around. But perhaps the most frightening revelation of epigenetic science is that even if widespread environmental changes were immediately instituted, it may take generations before the tsunami of autism will ebb.

CHAPTER 13

WHY AFFECTION IS MORE THERAPY THAN WE EVER IMAGINED. IT MAY ACTUALLY CHANGE OUR BODY CHEMISTRY!

COMING off the chapter of genetics and body chemistry I figured this was a good place to give this a quick look. Besides I think we need some positive energy after the scary prognosis of epigenetics.

The profoundly positive effects of affection are being revealed down to the chemical and even genetic level. Recent studies are showing that maternal behavior can actually sculpt the genome of offspring. As we look deeper into the effects of affection or neglect on the very young, this may illustrate why intense consistent therapies on ASD children are so important and why they are successful.

A study between nurturing and neglectful maternal rats was performed. Offspring were tested for any biological and genetic differences. First it was found that offspring of nurtured pups had lower stress hormones and lower blood pressure compared to the neglected offspring. The offspring were then switched to make sure there was no genetic predisposition to their hormone levels or blood pressure. Subsequent tests revealed hormonal and blood pressure changes correlated to the nurturing or neglect of the new parent. Furthermore, as the neglected offspring aged they were more prone to biting and other aggressive antisocial behavior. And not surprisingly, they were more inclined to age more prematurely due to their increased stress hormone levels.

The genes in the rat's hippocampus were examined; a part of the brain tied to communication and social behavior. Located at the base of the brain it has become of particular interest because it has shown to be much smaller in severely autistic children. The neglected rats showed distinct differences in the epigenetic codes compared to the nurtured offspring.

To tie the commonality between mice and men, studies have statistically proven that children who were abused, neglected and exposed to severe inconsistent discipline as children have higher blood pressure, anxiety, depression and drug abuse later in life. Furthermore, because of the higher stress hormones coursing through their bodies, they have a higher propensity to ailments such as heart conditions and diabetes. So once again we are seeing how the environment can instill profound changes down the generational line, in this case a positive environmental factor as basic as nurturing.

These preliminary tests reveal a parent's behavior may forever change their children's epigenome and body chemistry for better or worse. This may also shed more light on why autism is so malleable with intense therapy. Since a lot of evidence points that the epigenetic system can be changed for the worse, it may also be changed for the better through intense therapy and affection.

I also feel I have to bring the subject of corporal punishment back to play here. Though some believe autism requires this sort of discipline in order to shock or keep them in our world, the statistics indicate that if misapplied it can have devastating consequences. So once again, it's quite a balancing act on a razor's edge to administer corporal discipline for positive outcomes.

What am I saying here? I'm trying to get dads to realize how imperative it is to exercise consistent affection, (I think moms already knew this). Molding or in some cases even creating your child's affectionate behavior as rote and mechanical as the exercises can be at first can have profound physiological and chemical effects to lay the ground work for a more affectionate, balanced and loving child. This isn't just your Mom saying "affection is good for you, so give a hug every day." Scientific evidence is pointing out that your daily regimen of affection may permanently change the chemical formula in your children. This is why I believe it's so important to instill the AABA strategies as soon and as consistently as possible. The sooner you can ingrain that affection in their daily regimen the sooner you can see changes in their overall demeanor and behavior.

CHAPTER 14

HOLISTIC THERAPIES. SNAKE OILS, WITCH DOCTORS AND VOODOO OR HARD SCIENCE?

PLEASE note the information below is not to be considered or confused as medical advice. It is not to diagnose or substitute a consultation with your physician. This is intended to give you a base line understanding of some of the alternative treatments available out there and my personal experience with them. The goal here is when the time comes to talk with medical professionals you will have better conceived questions and not become overwhelmed. Be aware that some of the alternative therapies mentioned below use powerful drugs approved for "off paper" applications that may present very serious side effects.

Many of these alternative treatments have been called "The Cure or The Silver Bullet" by some parents and practitioners. But what are the treatments, how do they work and is there any proof behind the claims? This quick guide will help you understand the theory behind each treatment and allow you to make an educated and systematic approach to your child's therapy.

When I first heard of these treatments, I was quite the cynic. My view was that hardcore, consistent behavioral therapy was the only scientifically and statistically proven method to alleviate and reverse autistic symptoms. I felt if there were a proven pill or injection by now, a script from my neurologist would have been slicked off the prescription pad and slapped in my hand upon diagnosis. I'm not saying that the alternative methods below don't have merit or don't work; they are based on sound thinking where success has been proven on other ailments.

I hoped something would work on Little Em, but had little belief. I was trying to temper some overenthusiastic claims I heard out there or more importantly I was trying not to get my hopes up.

For example, I imagine you may have read claims that the Gluten free diet or vitamin B-12 injections miraculously freed their child's mind; that the child was suddenly speaking within weeks of the alternative therapy and began to emerge from their fog. I think many times what is commonly not addressed are the changes that took place months before the alternative therapies were applied. The minute parents discover their child's condition their behavior changes dramatically. Without even realizing it they have altered everything in how they communicate and curb behavior in their child. They make the child work harder at requesting something with speech or sign language. They learn better how to curb problematic behavior, incite eye contact and set up therapeutic play dates. An elite team of therapists rain down upon the child via Early Intervention or other avenues, but weeks or possibly months pass with seemingly little progress. Usually after some time the parents get brave and frustrated enough to try some alternative therapies like the gluten free diet or B-12 shots. A week or two later the child says the word everyone's been working on for months. The weeks or months of therapy don't get the credit. Instead the finger gets pointed toward the diet or shots.

It's nearly impossible to really know which treatment worked best for this typical example. The only way to truly test this is to single out each treatment and not provide the other therapies and then exercise other random placebo double blind tests. Then if there is progress the treatment would have to be immediately stopped and the child monitored for regression to determine if it was indeed 'the gluten free diet' or if the child's brain simply began to mature and develop its communication skills naturally on its own. Of course no parent is willing to put their child or themselves through such a narrow systematic experiment while their child's developmental clock is ticking. So the quest and market for alternative cures and therapies with continue to thrive.

As you can tell I approached these alternative therapies with a crooked eye and a cynical heart. By the time I wrote this I had exhausted most of the common therapies with little discernable success. I relegated the alternative therapies to "nice try, but no cigar", however, after deep reservations we decided to push through our exhaustion and disappointment for one final therapy. This therapy addresses the inflammation and allergy/autoimmune overreactions now being found with many autistic children. Just before Christmas at three and a half years of age we began to apply the medication. Within seven days Emerson began to grasp and repeat words we were saying to him for months – no years with no prior success. I'll never forget the first breakthrough on December 31st 2008. He was at the back slider wanting to outside. I got in his face and said "oooouuut?"

To my astonishment he looked at me as his mouth rounded out like a fish, "ouuss?" I was shocked. Never before did Emerson have the desire or ability to repeat a word on a first attempt.

"Out?" I said again out of disbelief.

"Ouuu." He repeated. I hugged him with everything I had and cried happy tears for the first time in recent memory.

Within three weeks of his first new word we got about a dozen more. I can't explain the catharsis that took place as I dine on the cynicism from my opening paragraphs. I do truly believe this last therapy made a profound positive impact, but I also don't want to take away that this must be combined with consistent therapy.

I also can't express more strongly as I illustrate below that having the right Holistic Practitioner is imperative to successfully and comprehensively see your way through the myriad of treatments.

MY FIRST VISIT WITH
A HOLISTIC PRACTITIONER:

I must admit I was not looking forward to going on this appointment. Jen had already been to five other nutritionists, holistic practitioners and dermatologists before this meeting. We were referred to specialists up to 500 miles away and when we cringed about the distance or cost we were browbeaten with, "well you should try everything available to get your son better." The nutritionist Jen previously met with simply took a look at Emerson and determined he had celiac disease before even testing him and prescribed the gluten free diet. We were even referred to an acupuncturist who was said to alleviate autistic conditions, allergies and skin problems. Beside the fact I'm against sticking my son with a multitude of hair like needles that can possibly snap if stressed or brushed wrong, my son wouldn't sit still in my arms even while cartoons were playing. Did they really think that was an option?

Most of these specialized doctors were not covered under insurance and as a parent we soon got the impression everyone had a hand out peddling their own version of snake oil. After all, there was no guaranteed success and just the consultation fees for most of these specialists ran from $150 to $400. We felt like we were throwing our money away, yet were guilt ridden if we didn't at least try. This was another great motivation I had for putting our experiences down in writing. If I had a guide to give me some direction of what to look out for it would have saved us a-lot of money, undue tears and time wasted before helping Emerson.

So we plowed forward or should I say Jen plowed forward. My skepticism was so high that I really didn't pay much attention to all the alternative therapies. My view was Emerson had this problem since birth and nothing was going to magically flip a switch on for him. As an analytical and skeptical guy, if I was going to go along with any alternative therapy I wanted a systematic scientific approach. I was tired of hearing about acupuncture or other shot in the dark therapies that didn't first run tests. I remember saying, "Show me where his brain waves are off, show me where his blood work or urine isn't normal and we'll go from there."

I had the luxury of narrowing my wife's search down as she did all the leg work. And I'll admit I would not have pursued this avenue at all if I were alone in this venture. This is where the determination and strength of Mama Bear shines through. Thank God she did or I truly believe now Emerson would not have progressed and would still be suffering from yeast build up, mineral malnutrition and the burden of high heavy metal levels.

Jen finally found Elaine Hardy, a Holistic Family Nurse Practitioner who came highly recommended on the D.A.N network. I decided to sit in on this one. Besides, we had to bring Emerson with us and I was best at handling him in an unfamiliar social setting (for the most part). As the initial meeting began Emerson tore her office apart, (see, I'm really good at handling him) but Elaine hardly batted an eye. Right away she spoke of administering a complete analysis of Emerson's chemistry. She wanted blood, urine, hair and stool samples. We would be checking for food allergies, heavy metal overburden and yeast build up from antibiotic use. Since we already knew he was allergic to milk and egg products she also suggested checking his blood level of essential minerals and other key factors that may be missing due to his limited diet.

Finally! – Someone who could give us a rundown, some statistics to look at and compare. When the results came in she had a very orderly approach to his therapies. She professed about being systematic to narrow down what was or was not working.

When his tests came back there were a few items that shocked us. His hair aluminum and intestinal yeast levels were off the chart. The blood test also revealed his vitamin D and Calcium levels were down in the malnutrition category. Now we could approach Emerson's therapy in a scientific manner, compare his mineral, yeast and heavy metal levels before and after treatment. This is something none of our pediatricians would even come close to doing with us.

I believe this is the only way to properly approach the alternative therapies out there; otherwise it will just exponentially increase the probability of wasting time, money and emotions. As a result you will give up too soon.

Not to go into excruciating detail of how each treatment was administered on Emerson, I would rather like to give a cursory list of therapies in the order in which we applied them – their applications and finally my experience for each one. As with any nutritional and alternate therapy, they must be individualized to the child's specific needs.

TREATMENT OF ECZEMA:

Though this is not a discussion for the treatment of autism, eczema is very common among autistic children. Little Emerson had cradle cap and eczema since birth. We used up the over the counter remedies and Betamethasone only did so much. We used oils in his bath; greased up his skin with all kinds of moisturizers, but Emerson incessantly scratched himself bloody. It got to the point where we had to constantly put baby socks on his hands to keep him from scratching himself open – especially when he went to bed as he scratched in his sleep. After going through the Betamethasone, A&D ointment and Cortisone cream with marginal results, an allergist prescribed Elidel to treat Emerson's acute case of eczema. I looked up this medication and discovered it has been associated with immunosuppressive related lymphoma and skin infections. Emerson already had all kinds of allergies, his immune system was in shambles and we had already dealt with a bout of skin infections. Furthermore there was a clear warning that long term safety of Elidel use had not been established. Very scary.

Elaine advised us that as soon as the blood work was done we should begin a regimen of Cod liver oil. She went on to say the cod liver oil not only moisturizes the skin from the inside out – it also was an excellent source of Omega 3 fatty acids – an essential component in building healthy nerve cells. It's also an excellent source of natural vitamin A and D. Vitamin A helps build the speech and vision areas of the brain. Vitamin D is crucial for normal brain development and if you look up Vitamin D on the web, there are now discussions on how a lack of vitamin D can have a profound effect on autistic children. As we later found Emerson was near malnutrition levels of vitamin D, we soon realized how much CLO would truly benefit him.

My Experience: First I want to address administering the 'icky oil" to children. We found the best way was to trick him (of course). We put it in his sippy cup and gave it a good shake. Yes it does separate but a good shake between sips will usually get enough down the hatch. There are flavored cod liver oils to help mask the fishy taste as well so it's not as bad as you may remember from childhood. We were referred to Twin Labs Norwegian because it's filtered in such a way to make sure there is no trace mercury.

To our astonishment Emerson's eczema cleared up in days. The alligator like skin along his arms and shins smoothed out and the embarrassing flaky cradle cap disappeared as well. I can't express what a relief it was to have this condition cleared up. Our concern that this would be a lifelong battle soon disappeared along with the flakes. We were also becoming hopeful the omegas 3's were having a positive effect on his nervous system. Sometimes the remedies Mom used to profess are still the best. The Elidel was promptly disposed of.

Gluten and Casein Free Diet: Gluten and Casein free diets are typically used in controlling celiac disease and help people with wheat allergies. Celiac disease is an autoimmune disorder of the small intestine caused by the reaction to the protein found in wheat. The immune system reacts in such a way that it attacks the villi (the absorption mechanisms) and thus reduces the body's ability to absorb nutrients. Symptoms include diarrhea, stunted growth in children and fatigue. The inability to properly absorb nutrients can lead to all kinds of problems. The longer it goes undiagnosed the more progressive the damage can be. An inability to absorb calcium can lead to poor bone density, children can have a delay in puberty, stunted growth and there is controversial ties to schizophrenia and other neurological conditions. It think of particular concern is potential myelitis – swelling of the insulating sheath surrounding the nerves. One does not outgrow celiac disease like other food intolerances.

My Experience: Testing for Celiac disease was included in Emerson's blood work with Elaine Hardy. I have no idea why our pediatrician didn't include this when we tested for allergies. Fortunately Little Em did not come back positive for Celiac, though he did show a mild allergy to soy which finally explained why his bowels were so irritable since we were using soy in place of milk. We knew he was allergic to milk, but had no idea about the soy. Once we put him on Rice milk his digestive system calmed right down. It became quickly apparent that Elaine's testing was starting to reveal all kinds of little things that were assaulting Emerson's body and best of all, we were beginning to chip away at them.

Though Emerson didn't show any allergy to wheat and tested negative for celiac, we still tried the gluten free diet to see if there was any difference in behavior. Now, a "gluten free diet" is nearly impossible. The term "gluten free" is not yet regulated on packaging in the United States so there can be certain amounts in anything labeled as such. Few tests have been done, but it's believed less than 10 mgs per day should prevent symptoms. It's an expensive proposition and rather limiting for your child's taste buds. After a month of spending triple the amount on food and attempting to match it with something he would eat, we finally abandoned this route since we saw no change in behavior.

Overgrowth of yeast in the digestive tract causing neurological poisoning: The theory is when yeast multiplies it releases toxins in the body that impair the central nervous and immune system. We were told some behavior problems linked to yeast build up are: hyperactivity, short attention span, irritability, and aggression. Yeast overgrowth is caused by Candida albicans, a yeast-like fungus present everywhere around us. Many autistic children, as with Emerson had many ear infections which put him on a regular diet of antibiotics. It's thought that frequent exposure to antibiotics and an inability to balance the gut due to other allergies (Emerson could not have yogurt due to his allergy to milk) amplifies the yeast problem. When we got back Emerson's results it showed yeast build up about 20 times the normal level. We immediately began a regimen to rid his system of yeast. Since it was so high we began with Nizoral then graduated down to Diflucan and finally kept a maintenance routine with nystatin.

My Experience: We were told to expect hyperactivity, diarrhea and possibly aggressive or irritable behavior as Emerson's body flushed out the yeast. It's said that as the yeast dies off it produces formaldehyde like byproducts that can create these side effects. Emerson did experience some diarrhea and irritability, which I would attribute to stomach cramps from the diarrhea. We waited the few weeks, but didn't notice any discernable difference in Emerson's "fog". However, after making the necessary changes in his diet and nutrition due to the findings from Elaine Hardy I did notice an improvement in Emerson's overall behavior. We got rid of soy, flushed out the yeast and supplemented vitamin D and Calcium. Emerson was soon sleeping better and seemed all around happier.

B-12 Injections: Known as methylcobalamin, vitamin B12 is a water-soluble vitamin that is very important to many functions of the human body. However, absorbing this vitamin for use is very difficult. Since many autistic children have digestion issues or are very narrow eaters; there is concern about absorption. B12 is required only in small amounts, but it is essential in maintaining many functions that center around the nervous system. Since autism is a neurological disorder the theory is to supply as much opportunity for the body to make use of this nutrient. Some believe the insulating sheath that covers the neurons is too thin in autistic children. Sort of like having a wire without enough insulation; it will cause lost signal strength and/or misfiring. Vitamin B-12 has been shown to help with dementia and increase mental focus in normally developed humans. It has a myriad of other benefits listed below that would seem to directly help some of the issues many autistic children are afflicted with.

- Maintaining a healthy normal nervous system.
- Creating a protective insulating fatty layer (myelin sheath) that covers all of the nerve cells.
- Metabolizing protein, fat and carbohydrates for energy.
- Helps increase energy levels - (may not be what you're looking for if your child is easily over stimulated)
- Enhances mood.
- Promotes growth in children.
- Helps in the absorption of calcium – This can be particularly helpful as many autistic children (and our son) are allergic to milk products. This along with a calcium regimen may help.
- Helps immune system function at its optimal level. (Another strong benefit for autistic children.)

Application: You will get a pack of pre-dosed syringes. They must be kept refrigerated and in dark packaging because light will degrade it. The syringes are very small (like those used of diabetes shots) and provide very little discomfort when applied. Typically parents will wait until their child is asleep, as we did, to give them the injection – usually in the hind quarters. The repetition is usually once every three days.

My Experience: Unfortunately we did not see the catharsis in our son that many other parents seemed to experience. We may have seen a bit more focus or cognitive/alert behavior, but as I mentioned before it is nearly impossible to determine whether the injections were the reason. After about six months we abandoned the therapy after not getting the results we hoped. This therapy was covered under our insurance, but our understanding that if it was not the cost would have been about $150 per month. I don't regret this therapy as there was really no downside to it other than a bit of discomfort for little Em. The additional B-12 could only help, and there was little risk of any side effects. It was also another avenue of therapy we could cross off our list and feel good about doing everything within our power to help him.

Chelation: Pronounced "Key-lay-shun", is the process of removing harmful heavy metals from the body. It is believed many autistic children have a lesser ability to naturally shed or chelate heavy metals from their systems due to a lack of certain chemical processes that most normally developing children have. A big concern is the buildup of ethylmercury (thimerosal) and aluminum from the vaccination shots. Aluminum has not been removed from children's vaccination shots and indeed aluminum build up has been tied to such things as Alzheimer's. After the hair analysis we found Emerson's aluminum level off the charts. Now Chelation is tricky in that you want to remove the bad heavy metal from your child's system, but the process will also leach the good minerals from their system at the same time. We were recommended to use DMPS or 23-Dimercapto-1-propanesulfonic acid. We administered it by rubbing a certain amount into his skin at night. It's a sodium salt that binds with various heavy metals so they can be passed through his system. It has a rather sulfurous (rotten egg) odor to it so it was another application we did right after putting Emerson to bed.

Dangers and side effects: As the process of Chelation removes heavy metals it also removes essential minerals. More specifically and improper administration of the wrong Chelation drug caused the death of a 5 year old autistic child due to hypocalcaemia or low blood serum calcium. This can be compounded by naturally low vitamin D levels which is required for calcium absorption. We were particularly aware and concerned about this due to Emerson's allergy to milk products as well as the blood work already showing calcium and vitamin D levels at the malnutrition level. I was not comfortable with Chelation and waited until the other therapies were administered and observed. We also waited until we made sure Emerson was getting proper supplementation and absorption of vitamin D and calcium.

My Experience: We were really hoping for some sort of breakthrough here. As with most parents, we marched down the list with little change and desperation increases. We kept hoping "this is the one" to make the breakthrough. It made sense for us that this might have a profound effect; Emerson was overburdened with aluminum and under nourished on Vitamin D and calcium. We thought perhaps realigning these imbalances would really help. But in the end we really didn't see any discernable difference. However, I'm glad we did it and knocked another treatment off our list. I slept better knowing Emerson's chemical imbalances were being remedied. I am also very thankful for Elaine's thorough and methodic approach. If not for her, we would have never realized Emerson's nutritional deficiencies or been able to correct them as Calcium and vitamin D are extremely important nutrients to developing children.

Anti Inflammatory Treatments: Some research shows evidence that brain tissue is swollen in many autistic children. The belief is this is an allergic and autoimmune reaction of some sort. In other words the brain tissue is being attacked by its own immune system and like anything else that's being injured in the body, the tissue will swell. The swelling chokes off oxygen, normal neurotransmissions and development, thus causing autistic symptoms. It's also believed the autoimmune response attacks and thins the myelin sheath that insulates the neurons. This stunts normal neurological growth and disrupts proper brain signal transmission. The theories of what substances cause this varies widely. Some believe it's an overactive immune response to the increased regimen of vaccines being pushed upon our children in large quantities over a short amount of time (the MMR vaccine is especially suspect) while others believe it can be as simple as milk or gluten allergy. Since Emerson had many allergies from the very beginning we felt it was worth deeper investigation. The treatments are designed to reduce the autoimmune response and reduce brain swelling, thus freeing up the brain to heal and function properly. To my knowledge there are three avenues towards this type of therapy. 1. Prednisone. 2. A combination of Celebrex, Singular and Actos. 3. Barometric Pressure Treatment.

Prednisone: After trying B-12, Chelation and Gluten free diet with little evidence of improvement, Jen and I decided to try the Prednisone for 10 days. Some parents decide for a three month regimen, but the steroid shuts down the adrenal glands and can have very bad side effects if not weaned off with decreasing doses over time to bring that function back. We reasoned that a ten day trail would be less risky and if there was a difference, we would see it.

My Experience: During the ten day regimen he surprisingly said "hello" when we handed him the phone (more like "ellooo"). It was a very exciting milestone, but we had been working on getting him to do this for some time and he already had a toy phone he would put to hear before this therapy. He went off after ten days and we waited to see if there was any regression. He still said "elloooo" when we gave him the phone but we weren't getting any new words so it was very difficult to determine any real beneficial change during therapy verses coming off. Again, did he just happen to make that progression by coincidence? We waited about two weeks and finally decided to try the combination of Celebrex, Singulair and Actos.

Celebrex, Singulair and Actos: There is an experiment by Doctor Marvin Boris regarding the combination of these medications to lower brain inflammation. Uses of these drugs are approved for: Celebrex: Non-steroidal anti-inflammatory drug. Singulair: Anti-inflammatory, allergy and asthma relief. Actos: is used in diabetic treatment to enhance absorption of insulin and reduce inflammation.

My Experience: I was not enthusiastic about administering this combination. I knew we were risking possible side effects with Emerson's digestion, but we were hoping against hope for the greater good to come out this. The next progression we were told, would be the hyperbaric chamber, but as I'll discuss below, we were not about to go through that.

We finally decided to administer the anti inflammatory combination. Within a couple days he seemed more 'animated' is about the best way to describe it, maybe hyperactive and also a bit more willful or stubborn. But he did seem happier as well and a bit more attentive to our voices. Then a very astonishing thing happened. Within seven days we had our first breakthrough with little Em mouthing the word "out." As I told in the story at the beginning of the chapter, I was elated to the point of tears and called Jen immediately. This spurred us on to try more words and again to our astonishment he was paying attention and attempting to repeat our words.

As I write this, I am apprehensive of over embellishing or calling this treatment a magic bullet. I hate to write of success that may not have the same effect on other families who read this, but I have learned a few things by Emerson's sudden progress. There's much more to this condition than I can ever hope to understand and that most importantly I need to keep an open mind. Jen and I still puzzle at his progress. Even his school therapists approached us with widened eyes, "Emerson has made unbelievable progress in the last two weeks! We should get together and discuss the changes in his therapy so we can all keep up." She wasn't kidding; the burst in his progression was that dramatic. About 20 days into the new anti-inflammatory combination Emerson still kept surprising us. One night I took him in the room that we normally do puzzles, but when I sat him down I decided to try something new. I touched my nose and said the word 'nose.' He mimicked me, and said "nose." I pointed to my eye and said "eye", he did the same, then ear and finally mouth. His words weren't perfect, but much closer than I could ever have hoped for and most surprisingly his gestures of pointing to the body parts followed along! I almost hate to admit it, especially after months and months of therapy, but I can't equate this catharsis to anything but the anti-inflammatory combination.

Some would say the next step is to stop the regimen and see if Emerson regresses. Sorry, but at three and a half years of age I finally have my son saying words though they are only echolalia. I'm not about to change anything back at the risk losing any of it.

Update: Four months in to the anti inflammatory combination and Emerson's progress has definitely flattened out. He's still repeating words and doing well with potty training and his PECS book, but it's not as though Emerson is heading down the Yellow Brick Road towards being cured. I recently spoke to a neurologist who admitted she has observed the same leveling off in other children. She mentioned the hyperbaric treatment. She did not believe it was a placebo effect, but that the kids tend to flatten out from sudden progression basically proving these treatments are not a cure.

Would I say it was worth having Emerson on these treatments? Absolutely! There were so many other things going wrong with his system that Elaine and her investigative therapy brought to light.

Hyperbaric Oxygen Therapy, or HBOT, is a medical treatment during which patients breathe 100% oxygen under hyperbaric (air pressure higher than sea level) conditions. This is done while sitting or lying inside a pressurized chamber.

How it works: Normally oxygen can only be carried to body tissues via the red blood cells. However, increased pressure produced in the hyperbaric chamber allows oxygen to be absorbed in the liquid or (plasma) part of your blood. This extra dissolved oxygen permeates body tissues in amounts that cannot occur even if you're breathing pure oxygen at normal atmospheric pressure. This increased oxygen promotes the body's own healing mechanisms and helps fight infection by killing bacteria that was otherwise very hard to get to. Medicare approves hyperbaric oxygen therapy for about 14 conditions. Autism is not one of them. Some of the approved uses for HBOT are :

- Decompression for the bends.
- Carbon Monoxide poisoning.
- Healing wounds that otherwise are not healing. This is especially good for diabetic's foot and leg wounds. It improves oxygen levels to extremities that don't have good blood flow which also helps diabetics.
- Bone infections.

- Gangrene.
- Flesh eating bacteria.
- Crush injuries.

The traditional hyperbaric chambers are hard shelled pressure vessels. Such chambers are capable of pressures nearly six times our atmosphere, however, for healing therapies they typically run 2 to 3 times atmospheric pressure. At these pressures, about 20 times more oxygen travels through the body.

Treatment: Treatment is recommended daily or every other day. The cost can range from $100 to $150 per session. You must travel to the site and spend about an hour in each session. Since all this can be very difficult to accomplish on a daily basis, a rise in portable HBOT chambers, for home treatment has emerged. These are usually referred to as "mild or soft chambers", which is a reference to the lower pressure of soft-sided chambers. They are typically made of a canvass material and only pressurize to 1.27 to 1.5 above atmospheric pressure or ATA. Those commercially available in the USA go up to 4 PSI which is 1.27 ATA. The soft chambers are FDA approved only for the treatment of altitude sickness and can run upwards of $20,000.

My Experience: Due to the lack of evidence and prohibitive expense, we have decided against pursuing this therapy at this juncture. I spoke with a few hyperbaric technicians in the field. Some told me the soft chambers didn't provide enough pressure to be effective, in other words, it's not enough pressure for the oxygen to dissolve into the liquid part of the blood stream. But when I asked at what pressure does oxygen infuse into the plasma part of the blood stream no one could give me a definitive answer. It is at 1.5, 1.75 or 2 times atmospheric pressure? Most facilities with hard chambers start their therapy at 2 times atmospheric pressure which is already above soft chamber capabilities. Also when speaking to these professionals about Emerson's condition and the treatment of autism, they were very candid in stating there was no scientific proof of any improvement through this therapy. However, I recently received an article regarding the most scientific approach I've seen to date regarding HBOT for you to review. They definitely went to a good amount of trouble to work through a double blind test to compare results. The only thing I didn't see addressed is whether or not they kept all study subjects from trying other alternate therapies while conducting this test. If Emerson were part of this test and got the Celebrex, Actos and Singular anti inflammatory treatment while in the HBOT test, it would completely skew the results. Otherwise the results do look very promising and it has piqued my interest to keep a close eye on any further tests. Below is the link for your review.

http://www.biomedcentral.com/content/pdf/1471-2431-9-21.pdf

The Final result: When I first wrote the closing notes we had yet to experience the profound progress from the anti-inflammatory regimen. I originally opened with, "To date, I do have disappointment, but no regrets in putting ourselves and my son through all the alternate therapies. We did not see any sudden catharsis in Emerson that many other families have experienced with their children. But discovering and addressing the issues like the high level of aluminum, dangerously low levels of calcium and vitamin D and an overburden with yeast were extremely important." However, I will still say we finally struck some pay dirt with the anti-inflammatory regimen. In the eleventh hour of our journey with alternative treatments we finally had the breakthrough I prayed for but never believed would happen. Though Emerson's sudden burst of progress has flattened out, I am still a proponent. I really didn't expect "a cure" and his sudden burst into speech albeit echolalia, is a relief as I'm more than grateful to get anything. All I am professing is the importance of finding a practitioner that can approach your child's therapy in a methodical manner and to keep trying with all that is within your emotional and financial power.

Finally, I would like to give kudos to Elaine Hardy, our Family Nurse Practitioner. Even if we did not have the great progress that we experienced at the end, she gave us something our pediatricians didn't.

She provided comprehensive before and after analysis of Emerson's blood, urine, hair and stool samples. Addressing Emerson's condition in such a thorough and methodical approach instilled confidence that we were doing all within our power to help our son and that is priceless. It eases some of the gut wrenching pangs that kept me up at night wondering if we were doing everything we could. If you are interested in more information on her services, you can visit her website www. holisticfamilyhealthcarepc.com

CHAPTER 15

HOW TO SUCCESSFULLY VACATION WITH YOUR AUTISTIC CHILD.

I can't tell the number of times I've heard of parents spending thousands of dollars on a vacation that turns into an utter nightmare. The intentions are wonderful and Dad's especially think this would be a great solution to light up his child's face and begin to bond. "We'll take him to Disneyland where he can meet all the cartoon characters, go in rides, and see the daily parades and fireworks. It should help with his problem; maybe bring him out of his shell when he sees his favorite characters" – if he has a favorite.

But from the moment they get to the airport terminal the nightmare begins. First the child melts down in the middle of the ticket line. He's so upset he develops diarrhea on the plane. It's so bad the parents run out diapers and clothes that he already crapped through. Everyone around is incensed. Even the stewardess snickers, "that's what Benadryl is for."

The entire trip is ruined for all as the child melts down in lines, becomes unresponsive at best or kicks and bites and screams in the middle of a show. Dad is brewing, *I spent thousands of dollars for this vacation and it's nothing but a nightmare.* Inside he starts pulling away and distancing himself. In his mind he's trying his best, but all his efforts seem fruitless. The static of his sour mood permeates the air and everyone is soon walking around with a dark cloud over head.

It's a hard and costly lesson, but just booking a conventional family vacation without preparation is not how to make things better.

But there is a way to make vacations the wonderful experience everyone's always dreamed – including Dad. Plan, rehearse, plan and rehearse. Without proper preparation and small stage rehearsals a good hearted gesture for a family vacation is no more than a formula for failure. Vacation time is a great thing to aspire for. It just has to be presented in very small doses and run as mini tests with your child. After reading the previous chapter, it hopefully gives you a better understanding of what your child is up against when it comes to sensory overload. Below are some suggestions to acclimate you and your child for a memorable (one you want to remember) vacation.

PRESENT VACATION SCENARIOS IN SEPARATE SMALL DOSES.

1.) Take your child to the airport: Walk him through the corridors, up and down the escalators. Stand in line, even if it's just for a bagel. Observe his behavior. If he can't wait in line, then you need to prepare for how one parent will have to keep the child out of line while the other waits. Food courts, escalators and waiting lines can all help you gauge just how ready your child is. If you haven't already read, look into the chapter of over stimulation. It will give you more insight and empathy to the emotions your child is experiencing and may help you better handle any meltdowns. There are other solutions discussed further down on this subject that reference booking tickets and such for children with special needs..

2.) Bring him on a bus before trying a plane: A bus is about as close as you can come to mimicking a plane ride. It's a steel tube with rows of seats and people in close quarters. Again, see how he behaves. Take him again and again until he's more comfortably acclimated. The best part is you can get off rather quickly and regroup should there be some sort of crisis.

3.) Take him to a 4H Fair, a local carnival or zoo: This mirrors the hustle and bustle of the larger chaotic amusement parks. If it turns into a complete debacle, you only lose a couple hours and a few dollars for admission. But the good thing is it gives you as a parent time to go home, regroup and strategize.

4.) Take him to a diner or food court to eat. We found out early on that our son was not one of those cute quiet little babies when going out for dinner. For a time we gave up going out for dinner, but after four years we slowly reintroduced the idea by starting with breakfast at a diner. Diners are much less formal and people seem to be much more tolerant of 'noisy kids.' Food courts at a mall are good as well. Both provide a relatively quick out should things not go well.

5.) Get a doctor's note if you're planning Disney: If your child has problems with lines the letter should include his or her diagnosis. It should also specifically state that your child's condition prevents him from being able to stand in lines for extended periods of time due to sensory issues. Other larger parks may have similar programs. It's best to call ahead and find out what you need to help make your family's experience as enjoyable as possible.

An example doctor's note:

To Whom It May Concern:

(Child's name) has been diagnosed with (autism) and becomes easily overwhelmed in unfamiliar crowded areas due to sensory issues. This hampers his ability to wait in long lines. If there are any special accommodations available to avert this problem, (name) and his family would benefit greatly. Any questions, feel free to contact my office directly.

Sincerely,
(Doctor's name)

6.) Search for travel agencies who work with special needs families. Typically they may have a representative at the booking counter in the airport on departure. Ask if they may provide your family with separate boarding on the plane to make it easier on your child.

7.) Present the doctor's note to a 'Guest Relations Cast Member'. Disney takes great care to provide the best experience for children with special needs and their families. They should present you with a "Special Guest Pass" that will enable your child and family members to 'queue jump' or jump to the front of the line. However, be prepared for the probable irate glares of the uniformed as you saunter past them with your normal looking child. I tend to oscillate on my feelings when this happens. One moment I feel a few hard glares should roll right off me. Other times I want to verbally berate them to tears or simply knock them out. Other dad's I've talked to have the same hair trigger. I think it's a natural reaction to a combination of frustration and parental defense. Do your best to let cooler heads prevail, remember it's a vacation and keep the focus on your child and family enjoyment.

8.) This is the time to make sure there is a clearly visible ID with your cell number and a brief explanation of your child's condition. Also include any medications he may be on. A wrist band or a lanyard that looks like a concert pass around his neck can't be missed. If they tend to pull it off, put it on your child's shoe through the laces and place in a way it can't be missed.

9.) Let your child be a child. If they like a particular ride and want to go on it six times, let them. It also helps to get to their favorite ride early before the crowds hit. Don't push the rides he or she isn't comfortable with. This isn't a testing ground; it's a place for fun.

10.)Allow time at the hotel pool to unwind, but don't depend on the life guards to watch your special needs child. Once again, this is where two parents are better than one. Take shifts watching him so one can relax. As in our case, our son looks and seems normal at first glance so others will be unaware of any increased danger so vigilance is 100% our responsibility at pools side.

11.) Walkie-talkies aren't bad idea if adults are separating to watch over another sibling.

With proper preparation a family vacation can be one of the great things to build lasting family bonds.

CHAPTER 16

POTTY TRAINING AND BATHROOM ETIQUETTE. START NOW!

"**J**EN!" I cried out as my eyes tried to make sense of the terrible sight stuck to my son's rear end. Emerson had just passed a small box of undigested raisins from the day before along with whatever else was in his intestinal tract. (Apparently raisins are to a child what a box of prunes are to an adult). I choked on the stench as Jen charged into the room with a condescending sneer. She efficiently cleaned Emerson's bottom while eloquently pointing out another typical male shortcoming. "You can gut a deer in the woods," she quipped, "but you can't change a poopy diaper by yourself?" She was right. I had no comeback as I was too busy struggling to not take another breath. Here's another example where women have this uncanny ability to work through the most explosive situation with cool collectiveness.

When Emerson was first born I had read articles of parents who potty trained their children between twelve to eighteen months. I daydreamed that was going to be me, but of course that was before his diagnosis. Now we had a nonverbal autistic two and a half year old to contend with. As a dad, I think having your child potty trained is one of those milestones towards humanity, one more step from baby to little person.

There are so many theories on how to potty train an autistic child. Everyone kept pressing me to ease up and wait "for when Emerson was ready", but as I believe is true with most dads or any parent, I wanted him potty trained sooner than later. I also learned by now that if you focus a particular task with consistency and discipline that these children can pleasantly surprise you at times. And if he wasn't ready (like candle blowing) then I would ease up and approach it again in a couple months. Furthermore, as I also learned with teaching him to blow out a candle, that even though I didn't think I was getting anywhere with all those months of repetition, the second time I tried seemed to come almost effortlessly. In my opinion "waiting for autistic children to be ready" before you begin any sort of training is a recipe for stagnation and disappointment. You should always keep testing the waters and pushing the envelope.

The impedance to attempt potty training sooner than later really hit me when I heard a couple nightmare stories. I remember talking to a dad who had a five year old who still wasn't anywhere near being potty trained and it gave me a shiver. We soon heard other stories of parents who had older children who still weren't potty trained. Later we heard that one teenager who finally got trained only after going to a new school that ratcheted down and focused. That told me he could have learned sooner.

So how and when do I begin to potty train a nonverbal autistic child? The answer to when: The sooner the better. You can keep defending reasons for delay, but potty training doesn't have to start with putting your child on the toilet. It can start as subtly as bringing them to the half bath to wash his hands every time they're sticky, also start bringing him to the bathroom every time he needs to be changed (this helps build the bathroom association with pooping and peeing). Develop familiarity and consistency with other bathroom habits. Have him put the seat up or down for you, flush the toilet when you're done and both wash hands together. Even if he's deemed "not ready" these things will make it much less of a stretch for them and easier on you when intense potty training begins. The answer to how: This has to be broken down into parts just like any other puzzle of autism and approached in small increments.

So this already answers the second question of "where to begin?"

By two and a half years old I began having Emerson follow me into the bathroom to start seeing what was happening. Some may argue the tactic of a child observing a parent going to the bathroom, but again there is such a limited ability to communicate that illustration is a primary means. Autistic children are visual and in my opinion this is the best teaching tool available.

Training a child to go to the bathroom should be about getting them to independently do all the things that come with going to the bathroom like raising the toilet lid, putting the potty seat on the toilet, bringing over the potty stool, independently pulling down their pants, etc, etc. The sooner you get your child involved in the individual finer habits of the bathroom, the sooner the part about actually going on the toilet can become an integral part.

Start out with him observing and participating in a consistent manner. Jen and I soon made the rule that every time one of us had to go, he was in there with us. Once we went, we showed him how to flush then started him in the habit of washing hands. Physically prompting your child to flush will usually result in one of the more fun aspects of potty training for them. As with Emerson, it was hard to keep him from pulling the lever too soon. Again I was using simple words and pointing for each command. I pointed to the handle while saying "flush", "on" for turning on the faucet, "wash" for washing hands. Due to his apraxia it wasn't until he was three and a half before he could start repeating the words. I had to physically prompt him how to put his hands together to wash. After a few months the chore began to set in and my hands could move further up his arms which allowed him to wash more independently.

When changing your child in the half bath, a way to get them to learn how to independently take their pants on or off is to only partially pull them down or back up. It will be uncomfortable and will naturally prompt them to complete pulling them up or down.

The PECS system may be of use here as well and it should be reviewed and integrated with a therapist who can build an individual system for your child.

Also note many autistic children have a difficult time discerning hot from cold. Once they master many of the aspects of hand washing, turning water on hot and cold is a good controlled environment to teach them. Emerson began learning at about three and a half by me saying "hot!" and "ow!" when putting my hand under hot water (not too hot). Soon Emerson was smart enough not to put his hand under the water, but would turn on the hot water and pull my hand under to see my overzealous "ow!" and giggle. All these little exercises can be administered way before he's 'ready' for potty training.

GETTING A TOE HOLD.

Many parents speak of some instance in which they realized their child may be "ready" for potty training. This happened for me one morning when Emerson was about two and a half. I got up and began to change his morning diaper. To my astonishment it was dry. Half naked and facing away, (just in case) I immediately picked him up and ran him down to the bathroom we had been using. That was the first morning he went on the toilet.

For another year we woke and immediately got him to the half bath as the first task of his morning ritual. His success rate varied, but we probably got him up to about 80% within four months which was right when he turned three and was about to start the new school. I tried to get him to go on the toilet throughout the day, but we had very limited and spotty success at best. I pressed the school to begin an intense potty training regimen and asked to be trained as well. They reluctantly agreed and began flooding him with fluids. They started out putting him on fifteen minute bathroom intervals with no diapers, but we weren't really accomplishing anything but wetting a dozen pair of pants a day. After two weeks of no discernable success we scaled back, but kept the morning ritual as well as the other bathroom chores going.

At three and a half we began to get echolalia and finally got him to repeat "peepee and poopoo" when changing his diaper along with the hand gesture (sign language). We discussed this with the school and decided to refocus on potty training again.

We waited for a time when there were no holiday breaks from the school for at least three weeks. We were given a chart and told to put him on the potty every fifteen minutes for no longer than five minutes at a time. We had to mark down each time we had a success or failure. There were to be no diapers and when there was an accident we were instructed to verbally discipline him with a firm "no" and as we were told, to "bring him back to the scene of the crime" and discipline him there.

Boy, this sure felt like ABA style of regimented intense training, praises for good behavior and immediate discipline for noncompliance.

The first night came and I can't express how frustrated and heartbroken I was all at once. There are certain times as a parent of an autistic child that you come to realize you have a real challenge on your hands. This was one of those instances for me. After four accidents in the span of half an hour I couldn't believe, 1.) Emerson wasn't getting it and 2.) How incredibly impatient and frustrated I was becoming. It was so hard to contain a controlled demeanor when he would pee in his pants sixty seconds after we had him on the toilet for five minutes.

In the span of two hours we went through about ten pair of underwear. But as frustrated as Jen and I both were, I had a feeling it would take hold this time. First off, every time we caught him peeing, we could tell he was upset by our verbal discipline. We were also catching it immediately. (One trick is to have him wear grey sweat pants - the color change is easily seen and the material tends to soak up the liquid better than other material.) By the mystified and upset look on his face it was obvious some wheels were turning in his head so we pressed on. Though this was absolutely no fun for us I realized this was working much like the other training we were doing. We were making our wishes relevant and the fact that he was now responding with the big lower lip to our consternation meant he cared what we thought.

I think as you become relevant to your child, as your worlds gel into one, I believe the child begins to develop other natural instincts, like not wanting to disappoint a parent or actually feel intrinsically bad when verbally disciplined. Before, when I was meaningless to him, I could have waved my finger, said all sorts of ugly remarks, made ugly faces and growled like a bear, but it would have had no effect on him. By this time, all the affectionate training and development of eye contact had given him the tools to better read faces and voice inflection. Now verbal discipline and facial expression to correct a behavior had so much more meaning and effect.

By the third day the school was having better success and I decided to try a little experiment, albeit a risky one. I noticed something over the summer when we would let Emerson swim naked in his kiddy pool. When he had to pee he would hold himself and seemed to be more aware there was nothing around his body to catch it. I also heard that parents of normally developing children would sometimes let them be bottomless between potty intervals to help keep the kids from having accidents.

I decided to try it while eating lunch in his high chair. It was resistant to getting wet and I was right there to monitor the situation while he ate. Furthermore, he was nowhere near the family room carpet or couch. Of course I failed to consult with Jen and had to explain his bottomless dress code when she sat at the dinner table. She reluctantly agreed, (only after holding herself harmless if there was an accident) so now it was all on me to make sure he didn't wander into a corner to do his business.

Luckily the experiment worked the entire night. By now we were in the habit of timing every fifteen minutes and he was in the habit of listening.

At just past three and a half years of age we have Emerson potty trained for the most part. The biggest hurtle we have now is getting him to communicate when he has to go in a public place. At home or school, he knows where the bathroom is and he will independently get up and go. But if we're out someplace or in the car he is still unable to independently tell us. He has never taken well to sign language and even though he can say "peepee," it's echolalia. We are still getting down on his level and reinforcing verbal communication every time he goes and it's an area we still need to work on.

Synopsis:

1.) Set up a bathroom ritual. Bring your child in with you whenever you go. Repeat the word "potty" while attempting to get them mimic the word and or hand gesture.

2.) Get them to begin to participate – have them raise the lid, flush and put the lid down. Give verbal one word commands while pointing. As your child progresses simply point to the object, like the lid or potty seat before verbally requesting. When they respond comfortably to that you can let them in the bathroom and wait to see if they can do the tasks without physical or verbal prompting.

3.) Start a hand washing regimen every time you go. This can take a-lot of effort and helps build on their task abilities for the time when they are ready for more focused potty training.

4.) Change their diaper in the bathroom so they can begin to associate the surroundings with potty. Here we also trained Emerson to throw away his own diaper in the garbage can.

5.) If you get some sort of toehold like getting them to go every morning when they wake up, hold onto it and try to build on it. For example start to put them on the toilet as soon as they wake up from an afternoon nap. It was over a year before we went from getting that toe hold to successfully being able to potty train him.

6.) Once you believe you have awareness, attempt an intensive potty training. For example, flood them with fluids and begin putting them on the toilet every fifteen minutes. Remove the diaper and have them wear grey or light colored pants so you can immediately tell when they have gone. When they do potty in their pants you discipline them 'at the scene of the crime' and then show them where they should have gone and place them on the toilet. If you are not getting anywhere you can retreat back to the lighter regimen and come back to it at a later date when you feel your child may be more receptive.

CHAPTER 17

IEP Meetings. Why it's so Important for Dad to be There.

B Y the 1980's the United States and Russia had been locked in a nuclear cold war for decades. When Ronald Reagan and Gorbachev finally conceded negotiations the famous words "trust but verify" hit the media. I think this is a great mantra to live by when preparing for your child's IEP. Better yet, go in with the idea of building bridges, but be prepared for war.

Welcome to the Individual Education Program or "IEP." The program was set up with all good intentions, to get parents involved with their children's education, but in many cases it has morphed into a place parents are told what their child's program will be. The parent – especially the single parent can be easily intimidated into not questioning the School districts assessments and without a doubt this is one place where dad must be completely involved.

IEP meetings are not something to take casually or to go in unprepared. View this as a business meeting. As a matter of fact view this as the most important business meeting of your life. After all, the amount of therapy your child will get is riding on it and the amount of therapy your child does or does not get will affect you and your child for the rest of your lives. Do your research, get your own independent assessments, even dress the part. I remember one teacher admitting to me how a father showed up in the multicolored garb and stained hands from his painting job. She admitted the school district committee walked all over him.

I believe the district therapists and counselors got into this profession with the best of intentions. However, by the time you meet them, many have been ordered to stand down by district supervisors to not disclose a child's true needs in order to meet budget requirements. Disillusioned, they have become another cog in the large bureaucratic machine. I have spoken with teachers who admitted they were told to 'shut up' by their superiors when it came to disclosing a child's real needs in an IEP meeting. 'This was for the greater good', they were told - to keep the district in the black and not pay for outside professionals. To me, this is no less that a chargeable crime.

Other than getting the initial diagnosis, this was one of the most stressful situations Jen and I have been through and I think the same goes for any parent. We found out there was no specific program for autistic children in our district. We read horror stories and the more I educated myself on the process the more worried I became. The "not knowing" if Little Emerson would be approved for the services we knew he needed put an incredible amount of pressure on our marriage and perpetually knotted our stomachs. We both had sleepless nights wondering just how much of a fight we were in for. We knew at his age this was "his window of opportunity" and we had to do everything within our power to make sure he would get an "appropriate education program."

So, let's get down to the nitty-gritty of IEP's. The first, most important and probably hardest thing to understand is where the district's legal and accountable bar is set when it comes to your child's education. When your child turns the age of three the district's level of obligation to your child's education is to provide a "free and appropriate education." The key word is "appropriate." The term "appropriate" was purposefully set up as grey and interpretive to allow for individual customized programs. Unfortunately this "room for interpretation" can be abused as well. To prevent this you must have the right mindset and approach the term "appropriate" from the same direction as the school. The term appropriate is not to be misinterpreted as "what's best" or what's even "most appropriate" so be sure not to use those terms in your discussions. Going into a committee with the approach of "what you think is best for you child" will fall on deaf ears and you will be succinctly shut down. Furthermore it will make it quite obvious you didn't do your research. I understand you're riding on emotion, that you're filled with angst about what your child is going to receive and you want what's best. But here's where I go back to the mentality of handling this like a business meeting. You must focus on facts and assessments when it comes to determining your child's educational needs. Period. Your instincts for your child may be spot on, but arguing with nothing more than a gut instinct while devoid of any reinforcing documentation presented through assessments will sell your child short.

The district will set up appointments for their therapist to assess your child's development and behavior at which point they will come back with a recommendation. I understand these are professionals in their field and they are held to that standard, but I honestly can't help but approach these assessments with a crooked eye. Now remember, these therapists are paid by the school district. Of course there's a conflict of interest, of course there's room for collusion. I know I'm not alone in feeling this way which is why the IEP process does allow the parent to have their own assessments completed for comparison. This is where you must make the investment to have your own independent assessments completed on your child. The reason I call this an investment is because it allows you to take an educated, reinforced position about your child's education and therapy structure. If you don't invest in independent assessments you risk forfeiting priceless therapy that your child so desperately needs. Losing out on therapy will cost you and your child for the rest of your lives.

I will say the experience from one state to another or even from one town to another can vary tremendously. When we first realized Emerson had autism we were considering relocating to Chattanooga Tennessee. Those plans were postponed as we emotionally recovered and tried to get a grip on what exactly our situation was after his diagnosis. By the time we were reconsidering the move, we had our own evaluations. The district we were living in had drawn the line and was going to do everything by the letter of the law. We asked if we could review their facilities and we were straight armed. But when I called an elementary school in Chattanooga and spoke to the principal she politely listened and referred me to a regional supervisor. I left a message with this individual and to my astonishment she called me the next day. She let us know how there would be potentially six schools in which Emerson may be eligible for. She asked if we could fax over the assessments and she would try to best match the schools that fit the assessment recommendations. I was flabbergasted. There was no standoff, no bureaucracy, no stating that they would first have to compile their own assessments before we could review their schools etc, etc. No, this woman invited us down. When we did make it down, she took the day to walk us through no less than five schools where we met with each principal and head teacher. We were allowed to ask questions about their therapy methodology, student teacher ratio, etc. To say the transparency and concerted focus on simply matching Emerson's needs to the proper school was refreshing would be a serious understatement. When we got back home we were still waiting for return calls from our district to review their program. Different mentality indeed, but the common thread is no matter how amicable or uncooperative the district, our own assessments came into play.

When your child is about to turn three, the district representative may come to your home or you may go to the school. Below is a list of questions you may want to ask to get a better picture of what they have to offer. Don't be surprised if they come to you with "twenty years of teaching and credentials" under their belt. But more specifically, you need to ask what experience do they have with autistic children.

QUESTIONS FOR INITIAL TRANSITION MEETING FROM EARLY INTERVENTION TO IEP.

1) What is your experience with developing educational programs for pre-school children diagnosed with ASD?

2) Explain the specific process that will be followed in formulating the IEP, goals and objectives, modalities of treatment and measures of success.

3) Who are the professionals who will be employed in my child's assessment?

    A.) Psychologist? (Y/N)
    Name:
    Experience, Years, Specialization:

    B.) Speech therapist? (Y/N)
    Name:
    Experience, Years, Specialization:

    C.) Occupational therapist? (Y/N)
    Name:
    Experience, Years, Specialization:

    D.) Behavioral Therapist? (Y/N)
    Name:
    Experience, years, Specialization:

    E.) Learning consultant? (Y/N)
    Name:
    Experience, Years, Specialization?:

    F.) Other professionals?

4) Are there any standardized tests which will be used? If so, what are the test names and why these particular tests?

Note to #4: This will be helpful information if you are looking to get your own assessments to compare with theirs. It gives them less wiggle room if you apply the same tests and you have different results. They can't say their assessment tests are more relevant or accurate. You will compare apples to apples.

5) Where will the assessments take place and will we be interviewed as part of the assessment process?

6) Can we schedule a date for the assessments in this meeting?

7) We have already conducted our own independent assessments and have yet to receive them. Who do we release the assessments to and who will be considering them along with the districts assessments? Can we meet with this person or persons before the IEP meeting to compare our findings with the districts or will this simply be compared at the IEP meeting?

Note: This gives you a great opportunity to see how cooperative or uncooperative the district will be. This also allows you to come more prepared. If you realize there's a great disparity or if they are becoming increasingly cantankerous about transparency, this should be your signal to get an advocate and attorney to accompany you!

8) When will the first IEP meeting take place? Can it be scheduled now?

9) Are there only a certain number of IEP meetings allowed? How many are usually done before a decision?

10) Who will be present at the IEP meeting? Names, job titles, experience?

IF THE DISTRICT ALREADY HAS A SPECIAL NEEDS PROGRAM, BELOW ARE SOME QUESTIONS FOR YOU TO ASK.

Basic Special Needs Program Questions:

1) What is the student to teacher ratio in your program for children with ASD?
2) Do you have year round program? If so, is there any time off in the summer?

Note: Even though there may be a 'full year' program, many schools still have a two week closing during the summer.

3) Does the school have a full day program? If so, what time does the school day begin and end?
4) What therapy methodology are they employing: ABA, Greenspan or some derivative thereof?
   A.) Why do you use those specific programs?
   B.) How long have you been using this program?
5) Is there a sensory room within the school facility?
6) What training have your professionals had with autism within your school system?
   (Here they may talk about overall educational experience. Make sure they stick to the subject of their experience with handling autism.)
7) How long has the specialized education program been in place for children with ASD?
8) What percentage of ASD children that have been mainstreamed by the first grade from your programs?
9) What is their measure of success for autistic children?
10) Do you have statistics on this success?

WHICH TESTS SHOULD I HAVE DONE AND HOW IMPORTANT IS THE NEUROLOGISTS REPORT?

Below is a list of things you should give the district assessors before they meet with your child. You should also get the list of specific tests the district will be using so you can get the same tests completed by your private assessors.

1. You want a general description of the child's disability by your neurologist. The neurologist may also be willing to put an opinion of the type and intensity of education he or she deems "appropriate or necessary." My experience is a neurologist report tends to trump all the other therapists assessments. Don't be afraid to ask for these things in the report. They usually have an idea what you're up against with getting your child the proper educational program from the districts and are very willing to help in any way they can. Listed are some things you may request be in the report.

   A. How does the child's disability adversely affect the child's education?
   B. What is the recommended teacher/student ratio and total class size. What type of teaching methods does the neurologist feel would work best and why.
   C. What are the specific amount of hours of particular therapies does the neurologist recommend per week?
   D. Is the neurologist willing to recommend a full day therapy regimen and extended school year?

As a parent need you need to have two things. 1.) Facts. Get your own behavioral, occupational and speech assessments done by a separate third party. Yes, it will cost about $150 to $450 per assessment and no your insurance will most likely not cover it, but this is imperative. 2.) If you experience any sort of resistance, evasiveness or indignant self righteous – "we know better than you attitude" when your district answers your questions then get an attorney. No if ands or buts. Yes, the attorney will most likely charge a $2,500 to $3,500 retainer. Ask family for help if necessary, whatever it takes. Make no mistake. This is the most crucial point of your child's education. Not high school, not college. I always think back to the first words from the neurologist who diagnosed my son. "Get all the therapy he needs now. Spend the money. Don't worry about saving for college because if he doesn't get the help he needs now, he will never go."

Request a copy of the districts assessment one week before the meeting. This provides you with invaluable time to review the documents and compare them to your own assessments.

Again, I can't stress enough that the district's level of obligation to your child's education is to provide an "appropriate education." Not what's best or what's even 'most appropriate' so be sure not to use those terms in your discussions. The minute you start to discuss 'your feelings, your instincts' or 'what you think is best' you will be run over. If they're sitting across the table with their professional assessments and you're on the other side with your instincts and what you think is best you won't have a chance. What you are attempting to accomplish by having your own assessments and neurologist report is to narrow down the grey area and make it ever more clear what your child's educational needs are.

If you don't agree with the district's assessment you are entitled to a free evaluation (IEE which is an Independent Educational Evaluation) from a private expert if you believe the districts assessment is inappropriate. However, usually time is of the essence. Your child may be missing the beginning of a school year or other critical therapy while you and the district duke it out. Having your own assessments allow you to immediately stick to facts and work in a business like productive manner right away. It will lower the chances of being postponed another few weeks as you wait for other assessments.

Now you may be hit with these weak excuses. "Well, we don't have a speech therapist, but we'll get one." Your questions need to go right at the heart of the matter. "Who is she, what's her credentials, what teaching programs does she use?" If they can't answer the questions to your satisfaction then sorry, no deal. If they don't have the programs and people in place for you to assess, then they don't have an appropriate program for your child. Period. You can ask them, "Would you buy a house without first seeing the blueprints or having a walk through? Would you even consider buying without knowing any specifics? I didn't think so. Sorry I don't buy fruit without inspecting it first, let alone my son's education program. How could you possibly expect me to blindly agree to a therapist you haven't hired or a program that doesn't exist yet?

Some say to go in with the approach of working with your district, to befriend them in a way. The argument is you may have to be working with them for quite a while and its best not to set up an adversarial situation. I'm not disagreeing with the approach, but don't let an understanding representative in your district lull you into a false sense of trust before heading into your IEP meeting. Do not fudge on this: Get independent assessments because you will be dealing with a committee of people who don't have your insight and will simply look to their paperwork to back up their position.

I'm not saying be nasty, but don't worry about making friends either. I'm saying stick to the game of facts to get your child an appropriate education. No one can fault you for that. Even the friendly folks in Chattanooga relied on our assessments in order to find the best fit. This is why it is imperative to have your own third party assessments no matter how amicable everyone seems to be.

The district may tell you they can't afford the therapy program being discussed. This is not an appropriate argument to the issue at hand and should be swatted down like a fly. It's as inappropriate as me telling them that I pay over $12,000 per year in property taxes and Little Em should get these services because I pay so much. What I pay is simply irrelevant. It's like saying I have more right to get my son therapy than the family renting an apartment down the street. It's not a viable argument for either side. It's about what your child requires via the professional assessments for a proper education. Go find the money, apply for Federal assistance. It is not your problem where the money comes from. As a matter of fact, that's what they're hired to do and it's their job to find the money.

They may say "your child's not entitled to that type of therapy." Or "it's not approved by us."

Be matter of fact. "If this is what my child needs as determined by the independent assessments then what's the debate?" Your child has a right to "an appropriate education" according to the federal government. Remember this is where you can refer to your evaluations or tell them you now want an IEE – Independent Educational Evaluation.

WHAT IS THE MINIMUM EDUCATIONAL STRUCTURE AND REQUIREMENT FOR AN AUTISTIC CHILD?

Whether a child is diagnosed PDD NOS, light or moderate autism, I believe at a minimum any educational program should be constructed on the three pillars listed below.

1) **An all day learning program.** No matter how "light" your child is presumed to be on the spectrum, thinking that a two hour program a day is sufficient to help a child diagnosed with autism is negligent. The one consistent element I have seen from any parent who will later make the bold statement that their child is "cured" from autism will admit their child endured a rigorous intensive therapy schedule of up to forty hours per week. I have yet to meet the parent who professes their child is cured after getting therapy a couple hours a day.

2) **A year round program.** If your child is out of school from June through September he will regress. Studies have shown regression is very typical of this condition and very problematic if it's

allowed to happen. Don't let your district experiment with "well let's have the first summer off and see if and how much your child regresses." Your child is not an experiment. Regression is a known condition to this diagnosis. It's like saying "well, we know he has diabetes, but let's not give him regular insulin shots over the summer and see what happens."

3. **One to one teacher to student ratio.** To get and keep an autistic child's attention requires the undivided focus and effort of a professional. The long term goal here is to get your child in more mainstreamed classes, but in the beginning he needs a one to one ratio. Do not compromise, do not give in. Use your Neurologist report and assessments to support your position. Any child truly diagnosed with autism will be utterly lost in the back of a classroom if there is a student to teacher ratio of 5 to 1, 3 to 1 or even 2 to 1.

I'm sure there will be those out there waving their fingers. "You're no doctor." How presumptive of me to generalize and diagnose minimum educational parameters etc, etc. But I believe these are the bare foundation pillars in which to design a program. These are children in the absolute beginning stages of learning. As a matter of fact these children must first learn how to learn and that's not going to happen if they are left to stare at the wall in the back of a class room while a teacher's trying to teach a half dozen or even two or three other kids. Their undeveloped minds are more open to change and therapy than they will ever be, but these are children enclosed in another world. This is the time they need all day, year round, one on one unbridled intensive therapy.

Synopsis:

1) Find out what tests the district will be conducting. Conduct the same tests for your own comparison.

2) Use the Neurologists report. Ask if they can diagnose what they believe the child needs in therapy regarding intensity, student/teacher ratio, amount of hours per week and year round. This is a prognosis from a physician and can have a profound impact on negotiating your child's needs.

3) Stick to facts when discussing your child's needs. Do not speak of what "you think is best for your child or what you want." Use the assessments to match the appropriate therapy schedule.

4) Research Attorneys. If you suddenly feel the need for one, you can pull the trigger quickly and get him involved.

5) The district's finances are irrelevant. If they cannot provide a program that is "appropriate" they are required by law to pay for one outside of district.

6) Autistic children are learning disabled. It will require one to one teacher student ratio, year round and all day classes. However, this is not necessarily a life sentence as with many other learning disabilities. Depending on severity it may take one year, five or even indefinitely, but therapy must begin with all due intensity and focus. The goal is to get your child mainstreamed as soon as possible. To think that someone is diagnosed as only mild to moderate requires less intensity means the child will simply take longer to get mainstreamed which means lost socialization among his peers and greater possibility of never fully recovering to his potential.

The bottom line, your opinions and gut instincts will be meaningless unless they are backed up with the factual findings of the assessments. You must approach IEP meetings with cold calculation, go in with eyes wide open and armed with facts.

CHAPTER 18

CLOSING

IT'S been less than the first four years of his life and even though little Emerson can't talk, he has already taught me so much. He was born to a self centered father who only thought of his own world crashing down around him when the diagnosis came. I'll admit autism cut me wide open and nearly bled me dry. It whispered terrible things in my ear and pushed me to leave, but its insidious effects backfired. Instead, I filled with resolve, compassion and purpose. Becoming a man with purpose grounded me in a way. The smiles and hugs that I worked so hard to instill in him now give me so much solace and peace and best yet, the tides have turned. Every smile, every glimmer in his eyes and giggling interaction slashes back at autism. This condition may well be with us the rest of our lives, but it's no longer the overwhelming monster that first overshadowed us in the neurologists room.

Jen and I have a journey ahead of us full of challenges and nuances that I'm sure we are not prepared for. However, I do believe, perhaps naively that the hardest is over. Since the day Emerson was born I've battled my inner demons as well as his, but we've emerged stronger and closer. I can now truly say he loves me the way I always wanted him to. After all the concerted energy, tears and support from Jen, our families and friends, I finally have before me a son who will look at me with round happy eyes and who comes to me for affection, hugs and the all important booboo kisses. He's so beautiful when he's looking at me.

The thought that I could have missed this by leaving when the chips were down is now inconceivable. I wouldn't miss those bright blue eyes or his infectious smile for the world. I beg all the fathers out there to stay in the game. As impossible as it may seem to break through the barriers of autism and steal your child back to our world, I say don't give up. By being there and trying, you already have him in your arms. He's too weak to crack autism's shell on his own. Help him break through, because when he does I'll wager his new found affection and smiles will instill the same delight as the day he was born and first put in your arms. After all, by helping him breakthrough, he is finally arriving into your world.

I wish you and your family all the best in your journey to heal.

Should you have any questions or comments feel free to contact me at Altruistpublishing.com

Appendix

Developmental milestones and Indicators of Autistic Spectrum Disorders

B ELOW is a list of milestones for normal development and behavioral red flags. I think that the milestones should be used as a loose general measurement since children do develop much differently from one another. Boys tend to develop slower than girls. What's more important is to compare behaviors considered to be red flags. If your child is falling significantly behind on the developmental chart and/or exhibiting any number of behavioral red flags I would highly recommend an appointment with a neurologist.

Normal Developmental Milestones

At four months:

1. Does he react or show interest in people's faces?
2. Does he react to parental emotion? For example does he smile to your excitement or smile?
3. Does he react to sounds or look for where they are coming from?
4. Does he follow moving objects like a ball or a favorite toy being moved back and forth?

At 6 months:

1. Is he starting to babble?
2. Is he animated or smiling when playing with a parent?
3. Is he showing proper emotion? In other words is he crying when unhappy and smiling or possibly starting to laugh when happy?

At 9 months:

1. Is he starting to mimic, to repeat a sound you make?
2. Is he starting to respond to giving and taking or things? Is he reaching for things on his own?

At 12 months

1. Should be able to babble at this point.

At 18 months:

1. Should be able to say single words.

At 24 months:

1. Should be able to put words together for short sentences.

Red Flags

1. Allergies and digestive problems early on. Colic, eczema, allergies to food.
2. Unresponsive to eye contact, actually avoids it. Eyes will turn painfully to the side or roll up if forced to turn in the direction of someone's face.

3. Repetitive behavior: Rocking back and forth. Waving arms, pacing in the crib.

4. Lining up toys and becoming very agitated if taken out of place.

5. Not playing properly with toys. For example, turns car upside down and spins wheels.

6. Over focused on spinning objects like toy wheels or fans.

7. Fits of rage: Especially when something was put out of place or when the repetitive behavior is disrupted.

8. Fascinated or interested in the mouth of others, while avoiding eye contact. May keep trying to touch a parents lips and mouth area.

9. Finds little need to play with others and ignores any interaction initiated by others.

10. Doesn't respond to his name even when parent's voice becomes obviously agitated. Wanders off or avoids playmate setting. May even run away from a playing group of children or be destructive within the play setting as he becomes over stimulated.

11. Improper emotional response. For instance, indifference to a parent entering a room after being away at work all day. Agitated to touch or closeness.

12. Doesn't wave hello or goodbye.

13. Toe walking.

14. Fails to point at objects or look to parent to communicate a need.

Bibliography

http://www.neurodiversity.com/library_chance_1974.html

Maternal Residence Near Agricultural Pesticide Applications and Autism Spectrum Disorders among Children in the California Central Valley

Environmental mercury release, special education rates, and autism disorder: an ecological study in Texas

http://www.ravenintellections.com/autism-pollutants.htm

See article: Epigenetics of autism spectrum disorders: (Human MolecularGenetics200615(ReviewIssue2):R138R150;doi:10.1093/hmg/ddl213)

Ghost In Your Genes 2006 BBC

ABOUT THE AUTHOR

EMERSON has a Bachelor's degree in Business Management from Rutgers University. As hobbies he loves to bow hunt, bike, fish, weight train and write. He currently resides in Califon, New Jersey with his wife Jen, his son 'little Em and keeshond Mugsey.